REAL LIFE ISSUES

Real Life Issues are self-help guides offering information and advice on a range of key issues that matter to teenagers. Each book defines the issue, probes the reader's experience of it and offers ways of understanding and coping with it. Written in a lively and accessible style, Real Life Issues aim to demystify the areas that teenagers find hard to talk about, providing honest facts, practical advice, inspirational quotes, positive reassurance, and guidance towards specialist help.

Other titles in the series include:

trotman

REAL LIFE ISSUES:
FAMILY BREAK-UPS

this way

this way

this way

is way

Adele Cherreson Cole

Real Life Issues: Family Breakups
This first edition published in 2006 by Trotman and Company Ltd
2 The Green, Richmond, Surrey TW9 1PL

© Trotman and Company Limited 2006

Editorial and Publishing Team
Author Adele Cherreson Cole
Editorial Mina Patria, Editorial Director; Rachel Lockhart, Commissioning Editor;
Catherine Travers, Managing Editor; Ian Turner, Editorial Assistant
Production Ken Ruskin, Head of Manufacturing and Logistics;
James Rudge, Production Artworker
Sales and Marketing Suzanne Johnson, Marketing Manager
Advertising Tom Lee, Commercial Director

Designed by XAB

British Library Cataloguing in Publication Data
A catalogue record for this book is available from the British Library

ISBN 1 84455 100 8

Typeset by Photoprint, Torquay
Printed and bound in Great Britain by
Cromwell Press, Trowbridge, Wiltshire

CONTENTS:

'You'll hurt and wish it wasn't happening to you. But it'll make you a stronger person in the end.'

Chloe, 16

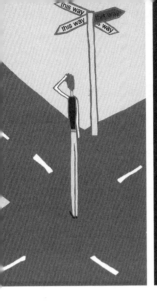

REAL LIFE ISSUES:
Family Breakups

ABOUT THE AUTHOR

Adele Cherreson Cole began her professional writing career in 1979 on the *New Musical Express* (*NME*). She went on to edit the young women's magazine *Look Now* and had a senior editorial role on *Cosmopolitan* in the 1980s. As a journalist and stylist she contributed to national newspapers, consumer magazines and specialist publications, writing on sex, relationships, health, beauty, fashion, interior design and travel, as well as news.

Since moving from London in the early 1990s she has managed a team of editors in a publishing company, lectured in journalism and extended her writing experience to include promotional material, websites, videos, presentations and books.

Adele spent five years in corporate communications at BNFL's (British Nuclear Fuels) power generation head office and latterly has worked in public relations and marketing. Her first love remains writing.

Adele lives in Gloucestershire with her husband and daughter.

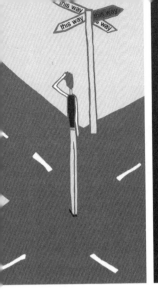

REAL LIFE ISSUES:
Family Breakups

ACKNOWLEDGEMENTS

Thank you to everyone who participated in the research for this book, particularly Paula Hall (Young People's Counsellor and Sex and Relationships Therapist, Relate). Thanks also to Judith Gunn, Andy Freedman, the Samaritans and everyone I interviewed, as well as ChildLine and YoungMinds for the use of their quotes from young people.

DEDICATION

For all my friends and relatives in their many different family circumstances.

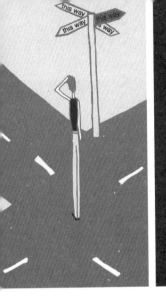

INTRODUCTION

Families come in all shapes and sizes – one size no longer fits all. Your parents may be married or not married. Your Mum or Dad may be a step-parent, adoptive parent or foster parent. But whatever your family unit looks like, it's disturbing when it starts to disintegrate.

By the time you are a teenager, family is no longer the centre of your universe: friends, school, college, even work, become the hub of teenage lives. As you become increasingly independent, Mum and Dad become the background to your life. But to Mum and Dad, you'll probably still be the centre of their universe and you'll rely on that to keep your life on track. They do matter, and it will matter to you when the foundations holding your family together shift, and major chasms start to appear.

Being a teenager in the middle of a family breakup is hard: chances are that your Mum and Dad have been together for a long time and your life is settled. As an older child, you may have come to realise that your parents' relationship isn't brilliant. But you still expect them to sort it out themselves – they are grown ups, after all.

'Whatever your family unit looks like, it's disturbing when it starts to disintegrate.'

You may feel pressured in all sorts of ways and pulled in all sorts of directions. You may feel that nobody else has ever gone through what's happening to you, that nobody out there knows what's going on, or cares, or can help. It may sound trite, but you're not alone and you don't have to handle it on your own. There are good, accessible organisations that can give you emotional support and practical help (see Resources at the end of this book). There are also things you can do for yourself; ways to increase your understanding of what's happening around you and inside you. That's what this book is about.

You may be concerned about how you're feeling and reacting, whether it's 'normal' and whether you can cope. Chapters 1–4 outline the stages you may go through and the feelings you may have about how your life is changing. You may not feel in control, but these chapters show that you can survive awkward situations, and even handle difficult issues to your advantage.

Chapter 5 gives practical information on what happens in divorce, including contact arrangements, as well as important issues like homelessness and abuse.

Chapters 6–8 deal with your new situation, whether it's shuttling between Mum and Dad at weekends, living with either Mum or Dad and facing up to their new relationships, or settling into a home life with a stepfamily.

The Resources section at the end of this book is mentioned throughout because it contains lists of organisations and websites that can really help you solve your problems.

The aim of this book is to inform and empower (as far as possible) young adults in dealing with their parents' divorce or separation. Even if there's nothing in particular that's a problem right now, it is useful to look at the stages, issues, feelings and outcomes in this book so you're prepared for what may happen in the future.

Read the quotes from people like you who have gone through the same thing. These teenagers are telling it how it is *for them*; so some speak of sad or bad experiences and others explain how they found that their family breakup wasn't really a big issue at all. Whatever their experiences and opinions, they will show you that you're not alone in all this. Unfortunately, many young people, just like you, are going through a separation every day in the UK – now called the divorce capital of Europe. It may be a sad fact of modern life, but family breakups are now the norm.

FACT BOX

If recent trends continue, more than a third of new marriages will end within 20 years and four out of ten will ultimately end in divorce. More than one in four children will experience parental divorce by the age of 16. Divorce rates in England and Wales (but not Scotland or Northern Ireland) are among the highest in Europe.
Source: Office for National Statistics

CHAPTER ONE:

WE ARE FAMILY
The emotional impact of family breakup

> '*When Mum told me Dad had left, it was so surreal. I couldn't take it in. At first I didn't believe her, then she started crying.*'
> **Chloe, 16**

From a young person's perspective, a family breakup is at best difficult to understand and adapt to, and at worst shockingly tragic. When a family breaks up, it affects everyone for a long time.

Family equals care, love, security and a home, and all those things are important. You may take your family for granted, even take advantage of them – but you need them, especially during adolescence. When there are constant uncertainties and insecurities in your life, it's great to have family to fall back on.

TEENAGERS AND FAMILY BREAKUP

Teenagers may expect or be expected to cope better than younger children with the news of a family breakup. Parents may need support

FACT BOX

In 2004, the number of divorces in the UK increased by 0.2% to 167,116, from 166,737 in 2003. This is the highest number of divorces since 1996, and the fourth successive annual increase.

Source: Office for National Statistics

from you (rather than giving it to you) or expect you to help with younger brothers and sisters. You may think that you will hardly be affected by the change in circumstances. But don't demand too much of yourself or allow others to make assumptions about your feelings and ability to cope. Sometimes being a teenager can make it particularly hard to handle a family breakup – take a look at the points below to see why:

1. As a teenager, you might be aware of your parents' difficulties, and you may feel you can help, intervene and make them see sense. But sometimes, the sense that a parent makes of his or her situation is to go it alone, or make a new life with someone else.

2. As a teenager, parents may view you as the next best adult in the house and think you'll be grown-up about them breaking up. You've been asserting your independence and pleading to be treated like an adult: they believe you can handle it like one.

3. As a teenager, you may be expected to care for younger brothers and sisters, providing stability and continuity in their lives, while the breakup is going on around them.

[4] As a teenager, you may feel you should support the needy parent. You may make decisions about your own future based on the needs of the parent you feel is most vulnerable.

[5] As a teenager, you may feel it's your fault. After all, you haven't been around much lately and when you have been at home, you haven't been that easy to live with. You may be convinced that if you'd spent more time with your parents, you could have held the family together.

[6] Now you're a teenager, Mum and Dad may make the announcement they've been putting off for years. Mum or Dad may want to pursue her or his own happiness before they're too old to start again. After all, you don't need them any more, do you?

HOME TRUTHS

These are all scenarios that could really happen; or they might just be played out in your head. Often, what you imagine is far worse than anything that really takes place. It's normal to analyse the situation and it's acceptable to ask your parents questions. Try to find out the facts first, and then work out how you feel. More information on how to cope with situations like those outlined above is given in Chapter 5.

Don't ever feel it's your fault. Your parents' relationship is something between them and if they are unhappy together it's because they can't

'When Mum and Dad told me, I realised I was going to have to live with one or the other. I knew what would happen from watching soaps. Except in soaps they have a lot more shouting!'

Maud, 16

work it out with one another. Sometimes two people just can't get on any longer. Maybe they want different lives to one another, have different values and perhaps don't like or respect each other any more.

Even if sometimes you seemed to be the cause of their arguments (for example, if they were arguing about different parenting styles or something you had done), you're not really the cause of their breakup: that's between them. It's normal for a teenager to want to take some responsibility, whether emotional or practical. But it's never appropriate for you to take responsibility for what is happening during the breakup. It's very tempting to try to help the parent who doesn't want the divorce or the one who will be left on his or her own, but don't take on that responsibility. You have to let them sort it out without butting in and it's not up to you to make things OK. Don't forget, they're the adults and you're still (and always will be) their child.

The crucial time between the ages of 13 and 18 is when the most change occurs in your life, and adding the upheaval of a family breakup can make the transition from child to adult very difficult. When you're 15, 16 or 17 your parents may feel you don't need them any more. After all, you can leave home or go to college and start your own life soon. But in reality, you probably feel more stressed now than ever before: you may have to deal with exams, schoolwork, career choices, a new job, a manic social life and your first real relationship. They may not realise how tough it can be for you and, initially, you might not either.

EMOTIONAL RESCUE

It's scary when your security and domestic stability are threatened and when there's a threat that important people may drift out of your life. It's normal to feel and think certain things. Dealing with those thoughts and feelings can be difficult, especially if your life as a teenager is changing too.

When families break up, people experience a range of emotions: shock, anger, confusion, frustration, fear and denial, as well as sadness. These reactions are real and expected. Often people in family breakups experience the same emotions as people who have been bereaved – because you may need to grieve for your lost family life. The diagram below shows some of the emotions that a family breakup can cause.

Phases of feeling

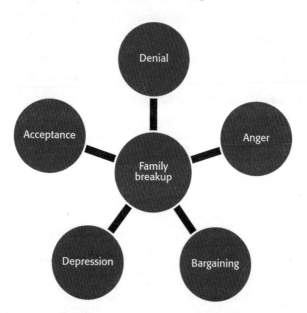

The path of bereavement and loss

■ **Denial** means you can't accept the reality of loss. In extreme cases it may be a complete denial, as if the person had not really left. There is also sometimes denial of the pain of loss, when people behave as if they are emotionally unaffected. This numbness is the way the mind protects itself from being overwhelmed by the shock of loss.

- **Anger**. This may be general anger with the world, fate or God, or an anger directed towards certain people – especially the parent who has gone. The anger may be a reaction to internal questions like, 'why have you left me?' and can lead to emotional, aggressive outbursts. This often happens immediately after the loss.
- **Bargaining** is when your mind refuses to accept what has happened and you may try to strike a bargain to get back what you have lost. This is a difficult stage – it may take you a long time to realise that things are not going to go back to how they were.
- **Depression**. As acknowledgement of the loss grows, depression can follow. This is the next stage of grieving, represented by an overwhelming feeling of sadness, loss and loneliness.
- **Acceptance** is when the bereaved person comes to terms with their loss, and is able to move on and accept the future. This stage is calmer, without the extremes of emotions of the earlier stages.

You are likely to experience some or all of these emotions over time. What's important is to realise that it's common to feel this way. You may believe your whole life has turned upside down or you may feel a sense of sad acceptance, but it's only natural to react to the family breakup. How you react and how your feelings are dealt with at the time will influence how you handle the process of separation.

Like a bereaved person, you may bury your response to your loss, outwardly appearing to accept the breakup. Even if you feel strong and certain most of the time, you need to make sure that the emotions you do experience are dealt with when you feel them. Leaving sadness or anger to fester is not healthy and it won't help you, or those around you, to get through the breakup or move on after it.

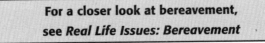

For a closer look at bereavement, see *Real Life Issues: Bereavement*

Allowing yourself to feel helps you understand that what you're going through is normal (the box below gives you a few pointers on how to do this). You'll recognise you're not crazy and you're not alone in feeling the way you do. It also opens the way to learning how to cope and helps you find a way to move on.

Confronting your feelings

How do you feel?

- Get in touch with your feelings. Try to recognise your emotions – do you feel shocked, hurt, betrayed ...?
- You may feel an emotion but not know why. For instance you could be angry, but not know exactly what you're angry about or who you're angry with. (It's normal to feel angry at the world when your parents split up.)
- Negative feelings can be scary, but what are you scared of? Your feelings won't kill you. You may be worried that emotions will spill out when you don't want them to, but the more you deny your feelings the more difficult they'll be to control.

What can you do about it?

- Try expressing how you feel in a secure environment. There are safe and healthy ways to express yourself: crying, talking to friends, writing down feelings, even getting physical (doing some enjoyable exercise, for instance).
- You may want to talk to a professional (a therapist or counsellor) to help you understand your feelings. Accepting help may be difficult but you may just need to chat to someone in the early stages of loss.
- Even if you feel anger, you can safely express it and benefit from it (see Chapter 2). Deal with anger when it's at a manageable level; don't allow it to build up.

What if that doesn't help?

- If you feel you can't cope, that your feelings are always near the surface or they're preventing you from getting on with everyday life, get help. You may need some advice or support: make an appointment to see your GP, call an organisation like ChildLine or the Samaritans, or speak to a Connexions adviser (see Resources for contact details). If you feel desperate, remember: you don't have to go through this on your own. Family breakups can be devastating and you'll always be taken seriously.

For a closer look at coping,
see *Real Life Issues: Coping with Life*

CHAPTER TWO:

WHY HAS THIS HAPPENED?
Facing up to the situation

Your reaction to the news that your family is breaking up will most likely be, 'I don't want this to happen; I want everything to stay the same!' Most children (of any age) in separating families just wish everything was 'normal' again. Even if your parents rowed, sulked or fought, you still may not be able to see why they can't work it out, and you might feel disbelief: 'This can't be happening to me!' Whatever you've experienced in the build-up to their decision, you may still not believe it has happened and you may feel that life isn't going to get any better. So when you get the news that your family is breaking up, here are some things you might find yourself thinking:

- This isn't happening, this is not for real
- This can't happen to me – how dare it happen to me?
- Mum and Dad don't love me any more
- Mum and Dad don't want me any more
- It's all my fault
- I'll never be happy again.

These are all normal reactions and can be worked through and resolved over time. Find someone sensitive and sensible you can talk to about how you feel. Have a look at the Resources section at the end of this book if you think you need further help.

> *'Most children prefer their parents to be apart and happy than together and miserable.'*

Remember, this isn't happening to you directly: it's actually happening to your parents. You will live with the fallout, of course, but your parents have made a decision about their relationship and their lives. They're separating because they don't want to be with one another any more, not because they don't want to be with you.

> *'There's just no point going off the rails. It's not your fault they're splitting up, it's their choice. You just have to make the best of it.'*
>
> **Matt, 15**

Research has shown that at the time of separation most children wish their parents had stayed together and hope they get back together. However, later studies report that once children are settled in separate, stable lives, most prefer their parents to be apart and happy than together and miserable.

CASE STUDY

Maud is 16. Her parents split up when she was 13 and divorced a year later. She now lives with her mother and stepfamily in a different town to the one she was brought up in. She sees her father regularly, although he lives 80 miles away. This is her story.

'I knew something was up when my parents started sleeping in separate rooms. They'd been arguing a lot before that. Then they sat us kids down and told us they were splitting up. I don't remember what they said. It wasn't a shock and I wasn't terribly sad, I just carried on as normal. I just assumed they would sort it out. They're adults. I trusted them. They made the decisions. There's not much you can do about it.

'I was 13 and my sister was 18, so she left home the first opportunity she could. She wasn't happy. She's always been 'Daddy's girl'. My brother was 20 but still at home and he was really difficult to live with. I think I coped better than my older brother and sister.

'I faced it every day and dealt with stuff as it happened. I didn't worry about it much. I think that was the best thing to do because my brother and sister were still angry and unhappy when they came back years later. They hadn't been through it day-to-day like I had. Because I was younger, I had fewer choices so I had to deal with it.

'Dad moved out and went to live with his parents. I knew I'd see Dad regularly, so I didn't worry about that. In fact, I've seen him a lot more since the split. It's nice to spend quality time with him. I suppose I see the best side of things. I just thought of all the extra presents and attention I'd get with two parents living separately! That sounds a bit shallow, but I just go with the flow.

'I think I get the best of both worlds. I have a close relationship with both parents. I'd like it if they were together and happy but they're happy now and that's all that matters.'

'I stayed in the house with Mum for a while and went to school. I was pleased to be in my own room and have my friends around me, but I wasn't too worried about where I went. I'd moved schools a couple of times and it wasn't a big deal. Then I moved from the city to the country with Mum and that was the most difficult thing to handle. I'm not really a country girl.

'I've got to know Mum's boyfriend and I live with them, which is OK. I like him. My brother and sister were really against him and it took a while for them to come round, but they're OK now.

'Now I'm older I see it as a good thing Mum and Dad aren't together. They weren't happy and I know my Mum is much happier now than before. I want them both to be happy. I just don't see how anything that's happened has been that bad. My parents live far enough away from each other that if one annoys me I can go and live with the other for a bit. I have more choices now. I'm more independent and more confident. I've grown up more.

'I'd have missed out on chances if they had stayed together. I like my life as it is now, even though it can be a bit boring going between two houses. But I think I get the best of both worlds. I have a close relationship with both parents. I'd like it if they were together and happy but they're happy now and that's all that matters.'

FACING REALITY

The sad fact is that nowadays two in five couples divorce and over a quarter of parents will have split up by the time children are 16 years old. You'll probably know other people who are coping with parents separating. How your future pans out depends on the decisions made by your parents and the input you have in them. Sometimes you'll be asked for your opinion but it may not work out the way you want: other times Mum or Dad will make decisions based on your best interests. Either way you have to trust them to do their best for you.

It makes the process easier for everyone if you know what's going on and why. Good communication can help the whole family adapt to the new situation. If you feel communication lines are clogged, start opening them up.

FACT BOX

The number of children aged under 16 in England and Wales who experienced the divorce of their parents peaked in 1993 at almost 176,000. This fell to 142,000 in 2000, and then increased each year up to 2003. About three million children in England and Wales have experienced the separation of their parents.
Source: Office for National Statistics

Opening up communication

■ **Talk to your parents**. Tell them what you're feeling. Tell them how you see the future.

■ **Ask questions**. Find out from parents, relations and friends what's going on and why. Try not to interrogate, though! Find out about your legal rights from websites (see Resources) or legal advisers.

■ **Be realistic**. Don't expect them to get back together. Don't plot to push them back together. Don't use emotional blackmail to try to get them to change their minds. It'll hurt everyone's feelings and harm your relationships with them.

■ **Look ahead and be hopeful**. It's a difficult time for Mum and Dad, so try not to be negative. Offer suggestions or solutions to help them make decisions. Don't go on about the past.

■ **Don't take sides**. Even if you think one of them is to 'blame' for the breakup, treat them equally. If possible, stay in touch with both parents.

■ **Talk to your friends**. Get everything off your chest. Rant and rave and let out the anger and sadness. Tell it like it really is. You'll feel better letting go of your emotions. Some friends may have been through it too and may offer advice from their own experience.

■ **Talk to someone neutral**. Sometimes there are just too many agendas with friends and family and you need an outsider to talk to. A trusted teacher or other adult can help put things into perspective. (Look at the Resources section at the end of this book for details of organisations that can help.)

Many of your fears, frustrations and questions will be because you don't know what to expect. Talking to people who've been through a separation will help, but knowing the process that follows a split will give you an idea of what will be dealt with and when.

What happens next?

If your parents are married, they:

- ■ May go to a solicitor for a Separation Agreement and put off divorcing until a later date
- ■ Will probably talk to a solicitor or a Citizen's Advice Bureau (CAB) adviser to discuss their options
- ■ Can either make decisions on their own or go through a mediator or solicitor to agree arrangements for children, finances and the family home
- ■ Will have to go to the Family Court for a Residence Order and Contact Order if they can't agree arrangements for you or your brothers or sisters (see Chapter 5)
- ■ Will have to prove that the marriage has broken down 'irretrievably' if they want a divorce within two years
- ■ Will have to be separated for two years before they can apply for a divorce
- ■ Can get divorced (if only one partner wants to divorce) if they have been separated for five years.

Sometimes it takes years for a divorce to be finalised. This is often because the couple involved don't start proceedings straightaway. If your parents split up, they don't have to get divorced: they can enter into a legal separation or just live apart until one of them starts a divorce.

DIVORCE AND SEPARATION

Divorce is the final ending of a marriage, enabling the former husband and wife to marry other people. If a couple want to divorce quickly, they have to prove the marriage has broken down 'irretrievably'. The grounds (reasons) for divorce are:

- Adultery
- Unreasonable behaviour
- Two years' desertion
- Two years' consensual separation
- Five years' separation.

Many people opt for a period of separation before getting divorced, or separate for many years. Some never actually get around to divorcing.

If the married couple are living apart, or with separate lives for two years, one of them can apply for a divorce simply on the grounds of separation, as long as the other partner agrees. If the couple have been separated for five years, either the husband or wife can divorce the other, without his or her agreement.

In theory, parents can divorce without agreeing any arrangements for the children or finances, but this isn't recommended by the courts. Usually final arrangements for the family, home and any maintenance that's due will be worked out alongside the legal divorce proceedings – which are pretty straightforward.

Divorce in England and Wales

- Although a divorce can go through in as little as four months, most divorces take about eight months. However, it can take a lot longer if negotiations over children and finances hold up the process.
- If your parents can't sort out a particular arrangement (like where you go to school) they can ask the court to make a decision.
- When people get divorced, both parents remain your legal parents, even if you don't live with them (see Chapter 5).
- In most cases, the parent you don't live with will be asked to contribute to the cost of keeping you. This is called **Maintenance** (or Child Support).

- The court or the Child Support Agency (CSA) can help decide how the parent you are living with gets Maintenance (or Child Support) from the one you're not living with.
- **Contact** is the term used for when and for how long you'll see the parent you don't live with. This includes phone calls and letters as well as visits and overnight stays (see Chapter 5).
- The **Decree Nisi** is an official statement meaning the court is satisfied the reasons for divorce have been proved. It comes before the Decree Absolute.
- The **Decree Absolute** is an official statement saying the marriage is over.

Legal separation in England and Wales

- If your parents want a legal separation they have to live apart (or they can live in the same house as long as they're not living as a couple).
- They can get a Deed of Separation to record the arrangements they've agreed on.
- A couple can separate and agree how to organise their finances and child issues without getting divorced at all. Divorce is an expensive and sometimes lengthy and stressful process and some couples decide not to get divorced until they want to remarry.

This is only a basic outline of the procedures in England and Wales (they are slightly different for Scotland) – see the Family Law Act (www.hmso.gov.uk/acts/acts1996/1996027.htm) for the full text. In England and Wales, however, the procedures are due to change – go to www.divorce.co.uk for more advice.

Divorce in Scotland

In Scotland, divorce actions can be brought in the Sheriff Court (similar to the County Court in England) or to the Court of Session, which is like the High Court in England. The law is set out in the Divorce (Scotland) Act 1976.

CHAPTER THREE:

INTERNAL INFLUENCES
Coping strategies for dealing with your emotions

Teenage boy: 'If I said what I feel they would call me a wimp.'

Source: ChildLine

Most children of divorced parents cope with the changes, settle into a new life and go on to live happy adult lives. Many young people will be philosophical about the breakup; if Mum and Dad are unhappy together, it makes sense for them to find happiness apart. As you start out on your adult life, there's no shame in being pleased for your parents in their new lives.

Sometimes one parent wants out, while the other wants things to stay the same. It's difficult for you to be fair and balanced about how you feel about Mum and Dad when one of them is unhappy about the situation. You may feel you need to look after the parent who feels deserted and you may want to blame the one who's moved on. But remember, your relationship with each of them is entirely separate from the one they have with each other. By the time you get to be a young adult, with relationships of your own, you may realise that what Mum and Dad do is their business and it's up to them to sort it out.

The key to dealing with a family breakup is trying not to get caught in the middle – but this is easier said than done, especially if you feel confused, stressed and upset yourself. This chapter will help you deal with some of the emotions you might experience and the knock-on effects they may have.

DEALING WITH FEELINGS

There's no doubt that the upheaval of a family split will affect you, even if you're positive about the resolution. The practical and emotional implications of sharing time between parents, moving home and school or seeing less of friends and extended family will change your life. These factors alone may make you feel sad, lonely, stressed or angry. It's reasonable to feel this way, and it is possible to handle your emotions before they erupt. Here are some ideas:

- Try deep breathing, meditation, yoga or pilates to handle long-term stress and aggression.
- When your emotions start to get too much, consciously relax your body. Concentrate on each muscle from your toes up or your ears down. Unclench your teeth and fists and uncross your arms and legs.
- Slow down your breathing and breathe from your chest and stomach.
- Listen to chill-out music to help you relax, or get into happy sounds and dance around your bedroom. Singing opens up the throat and deepens breathing, so switch on the karaoke or sing along to the radio. Steer clear of loud, violent music with thumping beats.
- Don't beat up pillows, scream, shout, or hit out to get rid of aggression – it only creates more adrenalin.

- Get some exercise. Hormones released after vigorous exercise make you feel calmer. Try swimming, cycling, running, dancing, athletics or team sports.
- Be nice to yourself. Look in the mirror and tell yourself what a great person you are. Be positive.

STRESSED OUT

What is stress?

Stress is a term used to cover all sorts of symptoms and circumstances but, put simply, stress is a physical reaction to an emotional response. It triggers a 'fight or flight' response in your brain, telling your adrenal glands to secrete the hormone adrenalin. Adrenalin causes an increase in heart rate and blood pressure, which is why you may feel your chest thumping at very stressful times. Other internal changes occur and another hormone, cortisol, is released, which affects your immune system. That's why you may be more likely to get colds and flu when you're stressed.

FACT BOX

Caffeine, sugar and nicotine are adrenal stimulants and can trigger a stress response even when there's no major external stress.

Source: www.fleshandbones.com

The physical changes prepare you to stand your ground or run, in what the body thinks is a dangerous situation. But in modern life, we feel stress because of exams, too much work, rocky sexual relationships, and when things go wrong at home. These are not dangerous situations, but they do cause stress. At stressful times (during a family breakup, for example) you can be constantly in this state. The strain on your body and mind can lead to panic and nervousness, which results in physical as well as mental symptoms as the stress hormones build up and cause damage. Symptoms of stress include:

- Fatigue
- Insomnia and waking early in the morning
- Tooth grinding at night
- Headaches
- Depression
- Anxiety and panic attacks
- Irritability and aggressive behaviour
- Low immunity
- Palpitations.

Long-term stress can lead to serious conditions, such as high blood pressure, heart attacks, stomach ulcers, irritable bowel syndrome (IBS) and menstrual problems.

Staying healthy

There are some simple things you can do to stay healthy when you're under pressure.

- **Cut down stimulants** such as caffeine, fizzy drinks and sugary foods, because they over-stimulate your adrenal glands and make you feel more on edge. Also cut down on alcohol and nicotine – these prevent your body getting the nutrients it needs.
- **Drink plenty of water** to prevent dehydration; this can include herbal teas (such as camomile or peppermint) or fruit teas. Dehydration puts added strain on the kidneys and can affect your concentration.

■ **Get good nutrition** because it helps your body cope with stress. Vitamins B and C, magnesium and zinc support the adrenal glands and boost immunity. Get these from a balanced diet or take a good multivitamin and mineral supplement.

■ **Eat regularly** – and don't miss breakfast. Avoid sugary cereals and have porridge, muesli, or even a boiled egg in the morning. A good protein breakfast maintains blood sugar levels, boosts energy, improves concentration and helps you deal with stress.

■ **Get enough sleep**. Teenagers need more sleep than younger children or older adults. Growth and hormonal changes happen when you are asleep, so give yourself a chance to mature. Stress can interfere with sleep patterns; you may find yourself waking in the night or sleeping longer in the morning. Try to get at least eight hours' sleep and go to bed and get up at the same time each day.

One of the most important ways to beat stress is to tackle it head on. If you feel constantly stressed out, after a while it will affect your mental and physical health and your ability to cope. Identifying which issues in your life are stressful and which are minor problems can help break the anxiety cycle.

Recognising when you are stressed

You can learn to deal with stress by developing an inner check, recognising when emotions and responsibilities begin to feel overwhelming.

1. Listen to your inner voice when it keeps saying 'I'm worried ...' This will often be in the evening, at night or when you're on your own. Stop thinking about the problem until daylight, the next morning or when someone else can listen.

2. Write down what is worrying you. List your concerns in order, with the biggest worry at the top. Work out why it is worrying you and what you could do about it. Look at how you might be able to

solve some of the minor problems further down the list so you can concentrate on what's really stressing you out.

3 Pay attention to nervous habits like hair twirling, nail biting, eye twitching and foot tapping. You may not realise something is on your mind but these are stress clues. Think through the muddle and single out the worry.

4 Keep a stress log to help you identify triggers and stress patterns. Try to interrupt the cycle of worry.

5 As soon as you start to get anxious say to yourself: 'STOP!' Substitute a pleasurable and positive thought. Think about a favourite person, a lovely memory or something you enjoy doing. Your mind will then focus on the new thought and your anxiety will fade.

6 Creative visualisation techniques also work: just thinking about yourself on holiday, being in the sun, being with someone you love or doing something you enjoy can keep stress at bay. Take time to visualise the scene you're in; think about the colours, the sounds, the smells. Mentally describe what's around you. This is relaxing and can draw your thoughts away from unimportant worries.

The diagram on the next page shows how you can use these techniques to interrupt the cycle of stress.

Tackling the root causes of stress

Once you've interrupted the stress cycle you can start to think calmly about your worries, work out how to solve your problems and prevent stress attacks. It's important not to dwell on things that are worrying you – imagining the worst can make you feel like you're going mad. Anxiety needs to be sorted out because it's important that you take care of yourself. You can do this in lots of ways:

■ **Talk it over**. Find a friend you can rant to about what's happening and how you feel. Counselling, psychotherapy and talking to someone

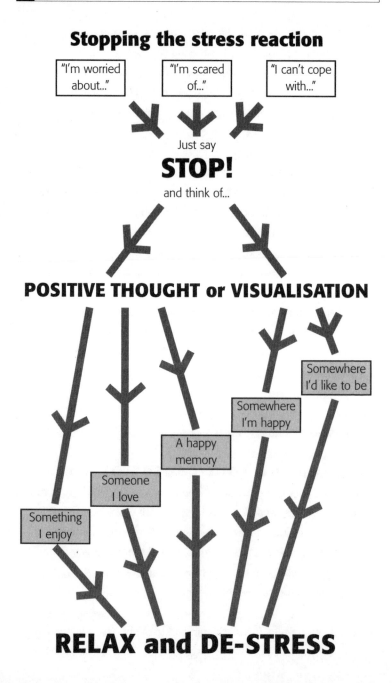

all help release bottled-up emotions and put problems into perspective. Talking things through may also help you find solutions.

■ **Release intense emotions**. Keeping a diary, journal or stress notebook is a helpful way to express your anger, sadness or disappointment. It's a way to transfer emotion out of your body and onto paper. This process helps you understand what's behind the emotions, too.

■ **Take a step back**. Imagine what's happening to you is a story or TV programme and put an actor in your role. Draw on someone from a soap and set the scene in Hollyoaks, Albert Square or Emmerdale. How would it play out?

■ **Draw boundaries for yourself**. With everything that's going on at home, can you really take the lead in the play? Can you really perform well in the football team? Work out what is going to be possible without adding extra pressure. Have ambitions but don't set unattainable goals.

■ **Ask for help**. You don't have to handle everything on your own. If you have too much to think about and sort out, think about how you might delegate something. Ask a friend, brother, sister or trusted adult. Could they take some of the strain off you?

■ **Create an action plan to handle a worrying challenge**. Divide the task up into manageable parts. Taking it one step at a time makes it easier and helps conquer anxiety.

■ **Set priorities**. There are times when your life might seem to read like a 'to do' list (Do the washing-up. Finish your homework. Study for your GCSE mocks. Read the book for your coursework. Practise that musical instrument. Get fit for the match. Shop for Mum's birthday present ...) You need to learn to decide which task is most important, and focus on that first.

> **For a closer look at stress,
> see Real Life Issues: Stress**

■ **Be positive about yourself**. Don't think: 'I failed the test because I'm stupid.' Do admit: 'I failed because the test covered work I didn't revise.' Facing reality means you're in control of changing the situation for the better.

SELF-ESTEEM

People who have low self-esteem are frequently very stressed. Self-esteem is about how you value yourself and see yourself in the world. Many outwardly confident people have poor self-esteem. Attractive, talented and intelligent people who put themselves in the spotlight can, deep down, find it hard to value themselves.

FACT BOX

The word 'esteem' comes from Latin, meaning 'to estimate'. Self-esteem is how you estimate yourself.

Source: www.freshknowledge.co.uk

QUIZ

Ask yourself these questions:

1. Do I like myself?
2. Do I deserve love?
3. Do I deserve happiness?
4. Do I really, honestly feel that I'm an OK person?
5. Do I blame myself for everything that goes wrong?

If you have low self-esteem you'll find it hard to answer 'yes' to questions 1–4 and will answer a definite 'yes' to question 5.

If you feel your self-esteem could be higher, you're not alone. Many people cannot fulfil their potential because they just don't believe they have any worth or anything to offer. Teenagers, especially, can experience temporary blips in their self-esteem as the constant changes of adolescence shake their self-belief.

How to improve your self-esteem

First of all: get real. That may sound simple, but believing that you're a fabulous, unique and valued person may not be that easy – especially if those closest to you aren't giving you the attention or consideration you need. Understanding who you are and what you have to offer is the first step – here are a few tips to help you put yourself into perspective:

- **Nobody's perfect**. You may not have the great figure of one friend or pass exams like another, but you have special traits and talents that set you apart. Don't think the glass is always half empty and you're a disappointment. Be positive and write a list of all the things that you – and other people – like about you.
- **To err is human**. No one gets everything right all the time. Let yourself mess things up occasionally – it's only natural. We learn and grow from our mistakes – they can be positive.
- **Taking the blame is not the same as taking responsibility**. If something does go wrong, why should it always be your fault? Look at situations realistically and honestly and don't always beat yourself up about it.
- **Impossible goals are just failures waiting to happen**. It's great to be ambitious and have aspirations, but be realistic! Don't promise (yourself or anyone else) to do something you know just won't/can't happen. You cause yourself unnecessary stress (see above) and you set yourself up to fall. Repeated failure just reinforces poor self-esteem.

■ **Respect yourself!** We all have the right to respect and if we don't respect ourselves, we teach others not to. Respecting yourself includes having the right to say 'yes' or 'no' and having your voice heard.

Just remember, you are an individual with rights as well as responsibilities. As a human being you have a right to be safe and healthy; and as a child (aged under 18) you have a right to be cared for. You have a place in society and your contribution to it is valued.

> **For a closer look at self-esteem,
> see *Real Life Issues: Confidence & Self-Esteem***

DEPRESSION

What is depression?

Everyone gets down now and then – it's only natural to react to life's highs and lows. You are bound to have feelings of sadness or even days of feeling sad during a family breakup. But depression is more than an on-off feeling of sadness and pessimism. When you are depressed, you are constantly low and see no way of ever feeling any different. Depression is a mixture of symptoms that can affect every part of your life, from not being able to sleep to wanting to commit suicide.

Symptoms of depression can include:

■ Being moody, irritable or snappy
■ Worrying about little things, or worrying about everything
■ Feeling lazy, bored or tired all the time
■ Not wanting to see anyone or speak to friends
■ Feeling numb and empty and not caring about anything (apathy)
■ Feeling you'll never be happy ever again

FACT BOX

About one young person in ten suffers from some type of serious mental health problem while growing up that affects their behaviour, the way they eat or sleep, their ability to study and/or their ability to get on with other people.

Source: www.youngminds.org.uk

- Feeling worthless; thinking that no one likes you or that people are talking behind your back
- Crying a lot
- Feeling life is not worth living and wanting to end yours (suicidal tendencies)
- Wanting to harm yourself
- Eating a lot more or a lot less than usual
- Experiencing sleep disturbances – waking in the night or having nightmares, sleeping a lot, or not sleeping at all
- Stealing things or getting into trouble
- Lying or making up stories.

'I can't sleep and I feel lonely all the time. My Grandmother died recently and she was the only one who cared about me. I live with my Dad but he hits me when he catches me smoking.'

Sean, 13 (Source: ChildLine)

Depression can last for months and prevent you from getting on with life. If you get to that stage, it's best to get specialist help from a psychologist, psychiatrist or psychotherapist. Your GP could refer you to a mental health professional or you could talk to a counsellor (see Resources in this book). The person you see won't judge you or think you're stupid or mad. They're used to talking to people who have all sorts of worries, and what you tell them will be confidential.

'I couldn't concentrate on my work. I was always daydreaming, and wanted to sleep a lot. I couldn't be bothered to do anything. Sometimes when I felt really low it was scary, and I'd start messing about at school, getting into trouble.'

Jade, 18

SELF-HARM

What is self-harm?

Self-harm can include cutting yourself, burning yourself or taking harmful substances. It can be done in private, dealt with privately and then covered up. Damaging behaviour like alcohol/drug misuse, eating disorders, unsafe sex and taking risks (such as dangerous driving) is not classified as self-harm but can be equally destructive. All these acts, including self-harm, show there are unresolved problems.

Acts of self-harm may lead to suicide or be motivated by suicidal thoughts, but there are many reasons why you might self-harm.

FACT BOX

More than 24,000 teenagers are admitted to hospital each year in the UK after deliberately hurting themselves. Most have cut, burned, severely scratched, bitten, scalded or poisoned themselves, or pulled their hair out. Research suggests that one in ten teenagers self-harm.

Source: Mental Health Foundation

Sometimes it may seem like the only way you can get attention or be taken seriously (a cry for help) and sometimes it can seem like the only way to cope with or show difficult emotions. It can be an expression of painful feelings (like pent-up anger, stress or depression) or lack of control over a part of your life. So in one way, self-harm seems like a way of getting relief. While many young people cope by crying on a friend's shoulder, self-harmers cope by injuring themselves. Just as many adrenalin junkies take progressively greater risks in sport, self-harmers take greater risks in the harm they inflict on themselves.

FACT BOX

Self-harm is becoming increasingly common among young people; 43% of people know someone who has self-harmed.

Source: Samaritans

Sometimes, those who repeatedly self-harm become increasingly tolerant of the pain and inflict more extreme harm to get the same effect.

Coping with self-harm

Young people who self-harm need emotional, and often medical, support. Going to your GP for medical advice and a referral to a psychologist or psychiatrist is a positive first step. Counsellors can also offer advice (see Resources for further details). If you're still at school and know a friendly teacher you can trust, let them know what you're doing and how you're feeling. No one who can help is going to tell you you're stupid.

If you self-harm and you want to stop, you need to find out what makes you do it and start to solve the problem before you can break the self-harm cycle.

Self-help for self-harmers

■ Counting backwards can help focus your attention and prevent a self-harm episode. Or focus on your immediate environment and think about something you can see, smell, hear, taste and touch.

■ Simple deep breathing techniques can be calming and distracting. Try yoga, meditation or pilates.

■ Make notes about your feelings and what's going on in your life when you feel the urge to harm yourself.

■ Write a list of all the people who can help you and places you can go to in times of desperation. These could be friends, family and teachers, or support lines such as ChildLine or the Samaritans. Make sure you write contact details for everyone on your support list and keep it with you. When things get really bad and you feel you cannot avoid a self-harm episode you must get in touch with one of these people.

Sadly, there is a link between self-harm and suicide, as the ultimate self-harm is to kill oneself. Sometimes self-harmers don't intend to die, but injure themselves so badly – by cutting a main artery, for example – that their wounds are fatal. Those who have self-harmed are at a greatly increased risk of suicide, which is why it is important for anyone who is self-harming to get support, even if suicide is not an immediate issue. All incidents of self-harm should be treated seriously and with care. If you are worried about self-harming, talk to a teacher or a trusted adult, or contact a support organisation with specialist advice like Mind, YoungMinds or the Samaritans (see Resources for contact details).

CHAPTER FOUR:

FEELING MAD, BAD AND DANGEROUS
Emotional management for coping with others

The sadness, loneliness, fear and uncertainty that are often reactions to a family breakup are understandable as you grieve for lost loved ones (see Chapter 1). But one of the most overwhelming reactions often experienced (by young people in particular) is anger. Ask yourself the following questions:

- Are you outraged that your Mum has asked your Dad to leave – or vice versa?
- Are you frustrated that you can't do anything about it?
- Do you feel powerless about your family's future?
- Are you fed up with Mum and Dad bickering over divorce, money and residency?
- Are you annoyed that your life – school, work, friends and family – is being disrupted?
- Are you angry that all this is happening to **you**?

Anger is a normal and acceptable reaction to a family breakup. After all, it wasn't your decision and you probably weren't consulted; yet you may have to change home, school or college. You may eventually have to welcome another family into your life. The disruption and transition can be unsettling and irritating. Staying cool while all this is going on can be difficult. This chapter will look at ways of handling anger and ways of making sure the negative emotions you feel don't have a harmful effect on your relationships with those around you.

MANAGING ANGER

Feeling outrage or anger is not always bad. If you have a real grievance it can propel you to do something about it; if you are being attacked (physically or emotionally) it can help you defend yourself. Anger only turns nasty when it's aimed aggressively at someone else or turned in on yourself. Being mean and cruel or feeling embittered are negative results of anger.

When you feel yourself exploding, try some of the following anger management tactics to calm down:

- Notice the tension building in your body. Make an effort to relax your muscles, especially in your fists, shoulders and face.
- Take several slow, deep breaths.
- Slowly count to ten.
- Slowly drink a glass of cold water.
- Recognise your angry thoughts and substitute them for calmer, happier thoughts and images.
- If you haven't eaten for a while you may be irritable because of low blood sugar levels. Make a meal or grab a piece of fruit; bananas are especially good because they are nutritious and release sugar slowly into your system.
- If you're tired and emotional, take a break. Try to get a good night's sleep or take a power nap – just 20 minutes can make a difference.

■ If you've been drinking, stop the alcohol and drink a few glasses of water. Avoid coffee as it will dehydrate you and hype you up, making you even more aggressive.

Young people often have difficulty controlling aggression, even in stable family circumstances. Growth hormones and emerging independence may make your behaviour towards Mum and Dad argumentative at the best of times. The way teenagers relate to adults – especially family – is often challenging. Just remember, it's not always easy for Mum and Dad to handle you, especially when they're feeling emotional, vulnerable or angry themselves. Most parents try to be understanding and make allowances for teenagers' behaviour; others are too caught up in their own emotions to be sympathetic. But now it's time for you to consider how they feel. Try to approach tricky situations in a positive and tolerant way, not in a challenging and negative one.

'It's not always easy for Mum and Dad to handle you, especially when they're feeling emotional, vulnerable or angry themselves.'

POSITIVE NEGOTIATIONS

The testing time at home is when Mum or Dad discuss (or argue about) the future. What's going to happen to you, your brothers or sisters, or the family home? It's likely to be your lack of control over what's happening to you that's most frustrating. However, there are ways of dealing with your frustration by trying to channel it into constructive discussions.

If you want to talk to Mum or Dad about some of the decisions and arrangements that affect you, you need to communicate coolly and calmly or you won't be taken seriously. Nobody listens to shouting and no one communicates when they're in a sulk, so make the encounter a positive one.

In discussions with your parents, you'll need to curb your impulse to fight and, instead, be thoughtful, tactful and tactical. Here are a few tips on how to achieve this:

- If you know you get emotional, count to ten as soon as you feel your blood pressure rising. Take deep breaths. Think about what you're going to say and how best to say it. Don't be tempted into a knee-jerk response to a controversial question.
- It's fine to say 'me' in conversations, but keep 'you' out of a discussion. Try saying: 'When this happens I feel like ...' rather than 'You always make me feel ...' Pointing the finger of blame and getting personal won't help. Keep the words 'always' and 'never' out of the conversation. Don't attack and don't be defensive.
- When negotiating with parents make sure your argument stands up. Think about it and practise it in front of the mirror if it gives you more confidence.
- If you know it's a difficult issue, tell them you understand the sensitivity of the subject. Try to empathise with them.
- Don't be afraid to let them know you've thought it through – prove you are mature enough to see the pros and cons. 'I've thought about this a lot and I can see that ... may be a problem, but if I ... it should be OK.' Go to them with a sensible solution.
- Most negotiations involve bargaining. Try: 'If you allow me to ... I'll ...'; or 'If I do this can I then ...?' Be willing to compromise and settle for something everyone's happy with.

■ Be reasonable. Don't expect to get everything you want at once. Be prepared to take small steps in the direction you want to go. Your parents need time to adapt too.

■ Say you've thought of their point of view – you may think it's unreasonable but you still understand why they think like that. Don't tell them they're being mean/stupid/unfair. If you don't respect their point of view, they won't listen to yours.

■ Be prepared for questions. If they ask a question you can't answer, don't go off on one, just say, 'I'm not sure about that, I'll think about it/find out about it and get back to you'.

■ Listening is important. Have your say, but let them have theirs too; then say what you need to. Don't shout them down.

■ Talk quietly and slowly; even if Mum or Dad's voice is raised. It will cool down the temperature and you'll be the one who looks mature and sensible.

■ Finally, if you can't get through a whole conversation without confrontation and if you end up saying things you regret, apologise. It really does help.

A FAMILY AT WAR

In a family that's separating, it's often Mum and Dad who are shouting and slamming doors. This can be alarming for children and teenagers. Normally it's Mum or Dad who takes responsibility, stays calm and manages the situation; but now they're both acting like unruly children. It can be difficult to handle the emotional atmosphere at home, especially for teenagers.

If you're the eldest child in the house or the one who Mum or Dad has taken into his or her confidence, you may feel responsible for keeping family life going. Younger brothers or sisters may start to rely on you for dinner money, help with homework, breakfast in the morning and a cuddle at night. Just when you're sorting out your feelings about the breakup, you have to help your siblings (and sometimes your parents) with theirs.

You'll want to help brothers and sisters through this and you'll want to see Mum and Dad come out of the divorce successfully, but you can't take responsibility for the happiness and welfare of the whole family on your own. No matter how mature and caring you are, it's just not your role and your parents may need to be reminded of that.

'Mum left and Dad's at work. When he's home he's so broken up he can't do anything. I have to get my little brother to school and to bed. With cooking, cleaning and shopping, I don't have time to revise for my GCSEs.'

Zach, 16

'Over the years I've been trying to help my brothers through the bad times. It was most difficult after Dad left, because he kept coming back, acting normally, then leaving again. We never knew what was happening and Mum was falling apart. I had to keep telling my little brothers that everything was going to be alright.'

Chloe, 16

Parents are often so wrapped up in their own crisis they are unaware of the pressure they put on their children – in particular older children. If there is something worrying you and you feel you can't cope, you need to tell them. You may feel that if you question them or complain, you'll rock the boat and make things worse at home, but they need to know how their behaviour is affecting the rest of the family. Remind them it's their responsibility to manage the breakup – not yours.

BLAME AND GUILT

'It's difficult not to take sides. I'm angry with Dad because he's made Mum so miserable. But I get annoyed with Mum when she bitches about Dad and his girlfriend all the time.'

Steph, 18

You may feel sorry for or responsible for one parent in particular. As a young adult, Mum or Dad may have told you more about the reasons behind their breakup than they would a younger child. Consequently, you may feel inclined to take sides if, for instance, one of them is withholding maintenance payments, had an affair or has a new partner to go to.

As one parent moves out and on to a new life, the other may lean on the next adult in the house – and that could be you. It's natural for you to want to see Mum or Dad happy and settled and less vulnerable. Just as they have loved and protected you, you may now feel the same obligation to look after them.

FACT BOX

Many children across the UK, some of them as young as ten, look after a parent – emotionally and practically. In 2004, the average age of 'young carers' in contact with specialist support was 12 and 50% of young carers were from one-parent families.

The difficulties and damage caused by such responsibility are understandable at a young age, but the stresses and strains of being the main responsible 'adult' in the house when you're an adolescent can cause problems too. Taking care of a needy parent, plus siblings, while trying to get on with your own life can be a tricky juggling act. In fact, more than a quarter of young carers who are at secondary school have problems (with behaviour or studies) at school. The stress of separation and divorce can be hard enough for adults to cope with, but if those adults lean unfairly on the adolescents in the family, the additional pressure can be enormous.

Sometimes it's flattering to be treated like an adult, to be taken into Mum or Dad's confidence and to be needed and trusted. But don't forget, you are still their child, and no matter what age you become, they will always be your parents. They have parental responsibility for you (see Chapter 5) and they shouldn't rely on you for their well-being and happiness.

If a parent wants to talk to you about the breakup, be sympathetic and listen to them, but try not to take it to heart or offer help that's self-sacrificing. It's difficult to control a runaway needy parent, but gently remind her/him that you are still a child and cannot offer support as an adult. If you want to help, make suggestions of where they can go for appropriate support (see Resources for a list of organisations). If Mum or Dad is in an emotional state he/she may benefit from talking to a professional, like a counsellor; if she/he is worried about money, housing or legal aspects of the divorce there is specialist advice available online or through the Citizen's Advice Bureau.

Remember:

- You are **not** to blame for your parents' breakup
- Keeping Mum or Dad happy is **not** your responsibility
- You are only responsible for your half of the relationship with your Mum or Dad: how they react or respond to one another (or to other people) is not your responsibility – or your fault
- Your individual relationship with Mum and Dad is completely separate from their relationship with one another. You are still a family (see diagram).

PARENTS BEHAVING BADLY

How well the separation works out is influenced by how your parents handle it, not you; it's how your parents feel and behave that shapes the way the breakup turns out – whether well or badly.

'Two years after they split up Mum was still bitter. There were problems and my Mum hated my Dad.'

Leo, 17 (Source: YoungMinds)

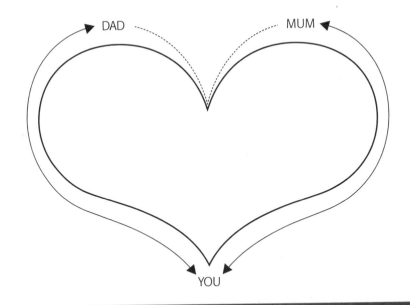

DAD ..... MUM

YOU

Even if Mum and Dad no longer have a relationship with one another, they are still your parents. You still have individual relationships with each of them. They are your family

Sometimes parents don't behave very well. Often, because they aren't thinking straight, they make bad decisions or have inappropriate expectations. They might unconsciously use their children to manipulate or injure their spouse. Sometimes parents are so angry with each other they will deliberately use their children against one another. You may be at the receiving end of their bad behaviour and it may be up to you to handle Mum or Dad when something they do makes you unhappy or uncomfortable.

The best way to tackle the situation is to let them both know how you feel about the way they're acting. Don't be afraid to give them some ground rules.

- Tell Mum and Dad that their happiness matters to you. Don't punish them for wanting to sort out their relationship or have a new relationship. But do explain that what they do and how they do it affects the whole family.

- Tell them you won't take sides. Even if you know about one parent's bad behaviour or another's neglect, try not to blame them. You probably won't know both sides of the story or all the relevant information anyway – there is no neutral source for you to get your facts from, so everything you get told will be biased one way or the other.

- Ask Mum and Dad not to criticise the other to you. Tell them you'll listen to practical information and decisions about the divorce but you won't take part in a slanging match.

- Tell them you won't be their mediator or their messenger. If they want to sort out divorce arrangements, they need to communicate with each other. If they're not speaking to one another, suggest they use their solicitors or a professional mediator, **not you**.

- Ask them if you can be involved in working out contact arrangements (see Chapter 5). As an independent teenager you have a busy school life and social life and don't expect to be treated the same as a younger brother or sister.

- Tell Mum and Dad their separation is their business and their decision and that you won't be responsible for what has happened or for making it better. Remind them they are still your parents and you and your siblings are their children. Let them know you will not take on an adult role in this breakup.

If that sounds incredibly tough, you may need some help in making your parents see sense. It may be easier to write down your thoughts, concerns and even demands, before discussing them. Send Mum or Dad (or both) a letter and ask for the opportunity to talk it over. Or email them if you can. They may sit up and listen if your thoughts are on paper; it's serious and you need to communicate.

Start your letter with something like: 'I wanted to write to you because it's easier to put my thoughts in order' or 'I wanted to write to you before talking to you so you have time to think about this as much as I have.' Try to avoid 'I have to write to you because you don't listen to me.'

'I've never told my Dad how I really felt. I'm still sad, angry and confused, even though it's been nine years since he left. I've thought about seeing someone but I've only ever gone as far as ringing ChildLine. My Mum forced me to go to a counsellor years ago, but I never said anything because she sat in on it. I saw a school counsellor a couple of times a couple of years ago and she really helped, but I've never had the courage to go back.'

Chloe, 16

Alternatively, you may want to talk to your parents with someone else present or representing you. This doesn't need to be formal – it could be a trusted friend or a relative. You just need an adult on your side to make a parent take notice. If your home situation is really difficult, ask for help from a social worker, mediator or counsellor (see Resources). Your tutor or teacher at school or college will help you make contact. If you feel in danger at any time, never be afraid to call the police.

Talking to an impartial (but professional) adult can help. Counsellors not only give you a safe outlet for your emotions but can also provide good professional advice on how to handle situations with adults.

CHAPTER FIVE:

FUTURE FACTS
Legal aspects of divorce and separation

Your emotional and physical well-being is very important and your Mum and Dad will consider your welfare when making future plans. They'll want to sort out practical issues – like where you'll live and how often you'll visit the non-resident (or absent) parent – with as little aggro as possible. If they can both agree and you're happy with their suggestions, then it should be straightforward.

However, parents may not agree and they may need mediators to help sort out these arrangements. These professionals help your parents negotiate with one another. If that doesn't work, then a judge in a Family Court may be asked to make decisions about where you should live or who you should see.

A legal separation or divorce is a formal process that usually works without too many hitches, but when parents can't agree, the law intervenes. As soon as action becomes official – when social services, solicitors, the Family Court or the council get involved – you may feel you have no control over what happens to you. But you will be asked your opinion and the court will always put your interests first.

FAMILY COURT

An application concerning you or your family might go to Family Court; it's not a criminal court, but one that makes decisions about children and young people. A solicitor may represent your parents, while a Children's Reporter or Children's Guardian will represent you. Your representative will be appointed by CAFCASS (Children and Family Court Advisory and Support Service). You may even be able to have your own solicitor acting for you.

If you're a teenager, you'll probably be asked your opinion. Being asked which parent you want to stay with most of the time can feel like a division of loyalties, but the court will want to know your wishes. In the end, the court or its representatives will decide what is best for you. Although the Family Court may feel like a scary place to be, it does act in your best interests and its aim is to make you feel less vulnerable.

It's unusual for parents to go to court to settle child contact issues. Most separating couples come to an arrangement on who should live with whom and how often you should visit the other parent. The options are either residency with one parent and contact with the other, or joint residency (where your time is split evenly between Mum and Dad).

Residence Orders (Section 8 of the Children Act 1989)

These orders decide where you live and with whom. A Residence Order:

- Gives someone parental responsibility for a child (see below)
- Lasts until the child is 16 – unless the case is exceptional and the court has ordered it to continue
- Can be granted to more than one person and can be made jointly to an unmarried couple

■ Prevents anyone changing the surname of or removing from the UK (for more than one month) a child without the agreement of everyone with parental responsibility, or an order of the court.

Contact Orders (Section 8 of the Children Act 1989)

These orders require the person you are resident with to allow you to visit, stay or have contact with a person named in the order. A Contact Order:

■ Is obtained by a parent for contact with his/her child
■ Can be obtained for contact between siblings or the child and other family members
■ Lasts until the child is 16, unless the case is exceptional and the court has ordered it to continue for longer
■ Can either be direct (face-to-face meetings) with a person or indirect (by letter, video, exchange of Christmas cards etc)
■ Can be specific about times, dates and arrangements for contact
■ Can be open, with detailed arrangements to be agreed between those involved
■ Can direct that the contact is to be supervised by a third person
■ May only be for a certain length of time.

These are orders of the court and if you don't comply with them you can be found guilty of contempt of court, which can have serious consequences.

Parental responsibility (Sections 3 and 4 of the Children Act 1989)

Parental responsibility is a legal term that refers to the rights, duties, powers and responsibilities a parent has for his/her child. More than one person can have parental responsibility for you, but people can also act alone in meeting responsibilities to safeguard and protect you.

■ The birth mother of a child will always have parental responsibility, unless the child is given up for adoption
■ If a child's father and mother are married to each other at the time of the birth, they both have parental responsibility
■ If a child's mother and father are not married to each other at the time of the birth, the mother usually has sole parental responsibility.

A father can get parental responsibility by:

■ Re-registering the child, naming the father on the Register
■ Drawing up an agreement with the mother (a parental responsibility agreement) signed by both parents and lodged with the court
■ Marrying the mother
■ The court making a parental responsibility order.

LEAVING HOME

A family breakup will inevitably mean you'll have to live with one or other parent and sometimes you may have to move house. For a few young people, it can mean you'll have to leave home altogether.

You can leave home at the age of 16 if you have the permission of your parents or carers. Sometimes this leaves 16- to 18-year-olds vulnerable, as many of the social support systems (like Housing Benefit and Jobseeker's Allowance) aren't available at that age.

This forced independence can be a problem if you're still in full-time education and have no means of supporting yourself. Although you can leave home at 16, you can't leave school and get a full-time job

FACT BOX

The Children Act 1989 brings Britain closer to the aims of the UN Convention on the Rights of the Child. It is about the care and upbringing of children. The Act was created with the belief that children are generally best looked after within the family, with both parents playing an active role. It lays down guidelines for care and responsibility, and states that the welfare of the children of divorced, separated or split families is the paramount consideration when making decisions.

until the last Friday in June of the year you are 16, even if your birthday is before that date.

Unfortunately, many 16- to 18-year-olds fall through the cracks when it comes to support from the government or local authority. The paragraphs below give an overview of what's on offer:

- Most single people under 25 renting from a private landlord can only get **Housing Benefit (HB)** to pay for a single room in a shared house. There are different rules for people who have been in care. Most full-time students and trainees can't get HB.
- You may be eligible for **Income Support (IS)** if you are aged 16 or over and are on a low income. You don't get IS unless you work more than 16 hours a week and have less than £8000 in savings.

- If you're aged 18 or over you may be able to claim **Jobseeker's Allowance** if you work less than 16 hours a week or don't work at all, but you have to register as being willing to work full-time.
- The **New Deal For Young People** is available for those aged 18–24 who are looking for work.

Source: www.dwp.gov.uk

HOMELESSNESS

If your family breakup leads to homelessness, there are ways to get emergency and permanent housing. You will be offered different options according to your age and situation.

If you're in the care of social services or go to an Advice Centre you may be referred to Supported Housing. This is available to a range of people with different needs and is provided by councils or housing associations. Young and vulnerable people are eligible for Supported Housing but there may not always be a suitable property in your area.

If you're under 18, you will most likely be put on the priority list by your local council and offered temporary accommodation while they assess you. Depending on your situation, you may be offered permanent council accommodation. A care order can be made for any child up to the age of 17, so if you are homeless and under this age social services can take over.

Citizen's Advice Bureaux (CAB) across the UK can offer you advice on housing and care. Look up your local CAB in the telephone directory or log onto their website (www.citizensadvice.org.uk). The housing charity Shelter offers expert advice online and through their helpline – see Resources at the end of this book.

FACT BOX

The council has a legal responsibility to provide temporary accommodation if you meet one of the following criteria:

- *You are homeless or likely to become homeless within 28 days*
- *Where you're living is only a temporary arrangement*
- *It's not reasonable for you to stay in your home (because of violence, overcrowding, poor conditions, or serious financial problems).*

Source: Shelter (www.shelter.org.uk)

ABUSE

Abuse comes in many guises – the fact box on the next page gives just a few examples. Abusive behaviour can be tormenting and bullying, physically violent or inappropriately sexual.

Domestic violence

Physical violence in the home is often referred to as domestic violence. Wherever violence occurs it is wrong and damaging to children and adults. Home is supposed to be a safe environment for the whole family, but some young people feel more vulnerable at home than anywhere else.

FACT BOX

Because it is invisible, emotional abuse is the most insidious and under-recognised form of child abuse. Five types of emotionally damaging behaviour are recognised: rejecting; isolating; terrorising; ignoring; and corrupting. Surveys by the NSPCC suggest that emotional abuse is the commonest form of maltreatment.

Source: NSPCC

Sometimes, during a family breakup, when emotions are high and tempers flare, domestic violence begins or gets worse. Children often witness physical abuse against a parent and feel responsible for protecting their mother or father. Often, especially during a separation, children and young people feel at fault for causing the violence.

The term 'senseless violence' is a common cliché, because like many clichés, it's true. There is never any sense or justification for violent behaviour – it is always wrong and should always be condemned. No matter what starts the argument or abuse, violence is never the answer to any problem, and it's never excusable.

If you believe that you or other members of your family might be at risk from violent or abusive behaviour at home, tell someone trustworthy and sensible about it. If you can't go to a responsible adult you know, like a teacher or a relation, contact one of the organisations listed in the Resources section at the end of this book for confidential

FACT BOX

One third of teenage girls experience domestic violence at home.

A fifth have been hit by parents (a quarter of them regularly) and a further 11% see their parents hit each other. Twenty-five per cent see their parents 'screaming and shouting' at each other. It makes them feel 'scared', 'angry', 'insecure' and 'confused'. But more than half don't think any of the above is 'domestic violence'.

Source: NSPCC Teen Abuse Survey of Great Britain 2005

advice and practical support. Don't forget – if someone is in real danger, you should get immediate help, or call the police.

Sexual abuse

Abusers are often those you look up to. They are adults or young people whom you trust and who care for you – like friends, extended family or babysitters. Most child abuse takes place in the home and happens repeatedly. When sexual abuse happens with a relation, it's called incest.

In legal terms, sexual abuse is when a person under the age of consent (16 years old) is pressured into sexual contact they don't agree to. This kind of sexual relationship is about power, not love. Here are the different types of sexual abuse:

- **Sexual assault** is when someone does something sexual you haven't consented to. This happens to men and women (over 16) as well as children. Sexual assault is usually an attack or a one-off act. It's a crime and should be reported.
- **Indecent assault** can be committed by a man or woman and is based on the assault being *intentionally* indecent. Any act of indecency involving someone under 16 is indecent (in England, Wales and Scotland).
- **Rape** is the physical act of having sexual intercourse (vaginal or anal) with a person (either male or female) without their consent. A man commits rape if (he is 14 or over and) he has unlawful sexual intercourse. It's rape if the person (at the time) does not consent to it, and if the attacker knows (at the time) that the person does not consent to it. (A man can also be charged if he is 'reckless' as to whether the person consents to it.) This may apply if the victim is drunk.

FACT BOX

One in six young people have experienced some form of serious maltreatment during childhood within the family. One in ten children and young people have experienced sexual abuse by people known to but unrelated to them.

Source: NSPCC (Cawson, 2002, Child Maltreatment in the Family: The Experience of a National Sample of Young People)

'I didn't know what to do, because I knew I'd always have to go home and face it. I thought if I could try not to think about it, squash it out of my mind it could be like it wasn't really happening. But stupid little things would remind me, make me feel horrible inside.'

Pete, 15 (Source: YoungMinds)

'Sometimes he would say "I'm doing this because I love you ... it's our special secret, OK?" I thought maybe it was just me. Maybe I just had the wrong feelings. Maybe all Dads are like that and it's just me who's weird.'

Scott, 14 (Source: YoungMinds)

Abuse of any kind in any relationship is always wrong and is not the fault of the person being abused. You mustn't be frightened to tell someone you trust what's happening. Sexual abuse relies on silence and the abuser is powerful only as long as it's kept secret. If you've been abused, here are some of the people you can tell:

- Teacher
- Social worker

■ Youth leader

■ Connexions adviser

■ Doctor

■ Priest, imam or rabbi.

Alternatively you could contact Rape Crisis, Victim Support or one of the other organisations listed in the Resources section at the end of this book.

If anyone touches you, talks dirty to you, asks you to watch them in a sexual act or in any way makes you feel uncomfortable with their behaviour:

■ Say **no** – firmly
■ Tell them to **stop** what they are doing
■ Tell them to **go away** immediately
■ Tell them you'll **tell** someone what's happened
■ Find a way to **get away** from them if you feel unsafe.

CHAPTER SIX:

SEEING THROUGH THE FOG
Moving on

> 'My parents have taken my wishes into account. My family is great. I'm sure there was stuff to sort out but they never fought.'
>
> **Joey, 18 (Source: YoungMinds)**

Everything may seem chaotic for a time as one parent moves out and arrangements are made for divorce or separation. You may have to move home or change schools or you might simply not know where you're going or what you're doing for a while.

As your life changes, it may seem that your emotions or uncertainty about the future hang over you like a fog, blinding you to the fact that there is the possibility of another life – for you and your family – when the fog clears. It may be difficult to be positive and hopeful about the future, but there will be a future – it just may take time to emerge.

It's easy to think that no one understands, no one has been through this before and no one cares. You may get down about it all (see Chapter 3), but there are lots of people across the UK in exactly the same position as you who may be able to share their experiences. Have a look on the internet (see Resources at the end of this book) for advice and to read about other people's experiences or speak to others at school or college who might be going through the same process. Share some tactics and have a good moan to each other!

SCHOOL'S OUT

School or college can provide a valuable support for you and your family – practically and emotionally. For example, if you are continuing your studies after 16 in a wide range of courses (eg vocational courses up to NVQ level 3, academic courses such as A levels or GCSE retakes at school or college) then you are eligible for the means-tested payment known as the Education Maintenance Allowance (EMA). This can help your finances.

What do I get from the EMA?

There are weekly payment bands of £30, £20 and £10 per week, depending on household income, plus bonus payments of £100 (worth up to £500 in total over two years). (These sums may change.) No other household benefits are affected and you can still have a part-time job. The money will be paid directly into your bank account.

In order to apply, you need to pick up an orange application form from your school, college, or local Connexions centre. Call 080 8101 6219 or log onto www.direct.gov.uk/ema. Your parents or carers have to fill in parts of the application form and provide evidence of household income in the last financial year. This will normally be the current year's Tax Credits Award Notice (TCAN) from HM Revenue and Customs.

> **For a closer look at managing your finances,
> see *Real Life Issues: Money***

Letting them know

Schools have a duty of care for you and will act on your behalf. If your parents haven't told your tutor what's going on at home, it may be down to you to explain. That can seem daunting, but you don't have to go into detail – unless you want to – just let them know that life at home is a bit unstable and you won't be at your best until things settle down.

At least if someone at school – your tutor or year head, for example – knows what's happening at home he/she can support your academic studies, especially if you've got GCSEs, AS or A level coursework or exams to complete. Don't use your parents' separation as an excuse for special treatment, sympathy or laziness, but be realistic about your ability to cope and accept help when it's offered.

If you're having real problems you may need to take it further and see a counsellor or social worker. Your school can put you in touch with the right people. Connexions advisers work closely with schools and, as well as advising young people about work and careers, they're trained to help with practical and emotional issues resulting from a family breakup (see Resources for more information).

Making the most of your time

Make the most of time away from the family hassle by enjoying your school or college life. If you haven't already, join some out-of-hours

'Make the most of time away from the family hassle by enjoying your school or college life.'

sports or arts clubs (although make sure you don't over-stretch yourself as this can add to your stress – see Chapter 3). If you really don't feel comfortable at home, do something positive after school with your mates. Try not to get stuck drinking, eating or smoking your way through the stress – it really doesn't help in the long run.

> '*I ran away from home at 16, after a childhood with no happy memories. I was brought up by my father who gave me no affection at all, even though he expected me to make breakfast and supper. School was the only place I was happy.*'
>
> **Ajirun, 18 (Source: YoungMinds)**

If you've moved home and there isn't a quiet place to revise, try to get as much done as you can during school time. Make use of the library or learning resources centre, or negotiate some study time and space with a teacher. No one will think less of you for doing this – in fact teachers are likely to be impressed by mature strategies to cope with what's going on in your life.

If you can't find study time in school, find a mate who will have you over. It's more difficult working in a social environment, as the distractions can be just too attractive; homework time can turn into Playstation, DVD, or just hanging out time if you're not self-disciplined. Try to separate the two and reward yourself with social time when you've completed your assignments.

YOUR RELATIONSHIPS

Time out is valuable if you're feeling stressed at home and at school or work. Not only do you need a distraction from what's going on in the family, you also need mates you can talk to. You probably know people who have been in a similar position. Divorce and separation are so common these days; many teenagers will have been touched by family breakup in some way.

Friends are there to have a laugh with and to cry with – whether you are a girl or a boy. Friendship is about give and take, so if you've offered support to one of your mates, here's your chance to get them to return the favour. You can:

- Use friends' experiences to help you with yours
- Talk over anything that hurts or confuses you
- Sound them out when you need to make a decision
- Cry on their shoulders when it all gets too much.

Encourage positive feedback and try to avoid a bitching session.

Your own relationships may suffer as a result of a family breakup: you may move away from your boyfriend or change school so you don't

'I can't see the point in getting married, it only causes grief. I have real issues with trusting men; I've never had a father figure when I've needed one and I don't think men are very reliable.'

Chloe, 16

FACT BOX

The divorce of their parents may lead adolescents to question their own ability to maintain a long-term relationship with a partner.

Source: P R Amato, 'Life-span adjustment of children to their parents' divorce', *Children and Divorce*, vol. 4, no. 1 (Spring 1994)

see your girlfriend so often. And because of what you have seen happen to your parents' relationship, you may just develop a jaundiced view of the whole love and sex thing.

Sometimes it may be difficult to feel positive about your partner when your parents are tearing their relationship apart. What's going on at home can influence your own relationships. How can you trust boys when your Dad's had affairs? How can you trust girls when your Mum is fleecing your Dad?

It's easy to be cynical about relationships when you see what's going on around you; people who have loved each other and lived with each other for years are now tearing one another apart. People do grow up and grow apart and what you're witnessing is probably the culmination of long-term dissatisfaction and unhappiness. Rather than be disheartened by what you're experiencing, learn from it and use your new wisdom in your own relationships. Remember, relationships take two people and the result is the sum of the two parts. It was the combination of both your Mum and Dad that led to the breakup.

Whatever relationship you're in, you'll be half of it and can influence your future. Here are some tips for a healthy relationship:

■ **Be choosy about who you're with.** You can't always choose who to fall in love with, but you can choose who you give yourself to. If you're feeling low or vulnerable, don't fall into the arms of the first person who offers tea and sympathy – or cuddles and sex. Keep your standards high – you deserve it.

■ **Put *trust* high up on your priority list** when committing to a relationship. If you can't trust your partner – to be faithful, to be honest, to cherish you – it doesn't matter how fit he/she is, the relationship is on shaky ground from the start.

■ **Don't be too needy** – it'll make you vulnerable. If you've never had a mother or father figure to rely on, try not to be too desperate for the attention of the opposite sex. You'll leave yourself open to hurt and abuse.

■ **Try to deal with issues as they come up**, whatever the circumstances, because leaving bad feeling to fester creates long-term problems.

■ **Be honest**. It's OK to say, 'when you did ... it made me feel ...' Your feelings may not be logical, but they are valid.

> **For a closer look at relationships,**
> **see *Real Life Issues: Sex and Relationships***

GRANDPARENTING

Grandparents can have a rough deal during a family breakup: they may have to give emotional support to their son or daughter, they may have to give practical support (for example by looking after the grandchildren) and they may have to give financial support to a lone parent. And if their grandchildren move away to live with the unrelated parent, they may have less contact with them than before.

Until recently grandparents had no status in the divorce system and sometimes the very people who spent most time with children as they were growing up were completely cut off from them as the family split. Nowadays everyone agrees how important it is for grandparents to have contact. Often, a grandparent's home is the ideal place for children to meet their non-resident parent.

Don't leave grandparents out of your life just because they're the parents of your parent who split. Try not to blame your grandparents for the behaviour of your Mum or Dad. Your parents are adults and make their own decisions. You may feel grandparents have taken sides, but it's natural for them to be loyal to their own child – they're just being caring parents, and even if they have reservations about how their son or daughter has behaved, they are unlikely to share these with you.

If you're angry with Gran or Grandad for their attitude towards Mum or Dad, go and speak to them about it. Explain what's going on and how it makes you feel; give them the opportunity for a better understanding of the situation. If you don't like it when they moan about Mum or Dad, tell them to stop. Your relationship with them should be completely separate from what's going on between your parents; occasionally you may have to gently remind them of that.

Grandparents can be very useful in a family breakup ...

- ■ They can provide neutral territory for meetings
- ■ They can act as your informal advocate, speaking to Mum or Dad or to your school on your behalf
- ■ They can provide a second opinion or just a caring ear to listen to your worries.

'When my Dad left, Mum didn't want us to see Gran and Grandpa. She was so mad at him. And they were angry too, at first. Then Gran got in touch and spoke to her and they both agreed it wasn't fair to us. So now, we see them just as much as we used to, and it's good. We see Dad round theirs too and that's nice.'

Amy, 13 (Source: Parentline Plus)

CHAPTER SEVEN:

LIVING WITH ONE PARENT
New lifestyles

There's no need to feel alone if you're living with a lone parent. Nowadays a quarter of all children live with just their Mum or their Dad. The traditional family of 2.4 children and two parents is no longer the norm – despite what cheesy sitcoms and American TV series would suggest!

Although the media would have us believe that the UK is awash with teen mums in council housing, in fact the majority of lone parents are older mums. They're mostly looking after children on their own because of a relationship breakup.

You may be, or about to be, in a similar situation. As we saw in Chapter 2, wanting things to stay as they are (ie having two parents at home) may be your ideal solution – but, like it or not, things are going to change. This chapter will look at ways of coping with that change and making the best of life.

'There's no need to feel alone if you're living with a lone parent.'

It can be nice having Mum or Dad all to yourself, especially if you still have a close relationship with the parent you don't live with. This is the ideal, but it doesn't always happen – or not immediately. Like all relationships, split parenthood takes practice and hard work and there will be certain pain barriers to crash through on the way. You might need to be patient while Mum and Dad are working out their new lives.

FACT BOX

There are 1.8 million one-parent families in Britain and they care for nearly 3 million children. About nine out of ten lone parents are women. The median age for a lone parent is 35. Lone parenthood lasts on average about five years. In 2004, one in four dependent children lived in one-parent families. This was an increase from one in 14 in 1972.

Source: Office for National Statistics

THE DOUBLE LIFE

Arrive at any service station on a major motorway in Britain on a Friday evening or Sunday afternoon and you'll witness the swapping of children, luggage, Christmas presents, homework, bikes and, occasionally, family pets. It's a representative image of families today as young people of all ages cope with dual lives, to-ing and fro-ing between Mum and Dad.

> *'The divorce hasn't been a big problem to me. Provided parents act properly, divorce shouldn't be a problem.'*
>
> **Jake, 14 (Source: YoungMinds)**

At first this double life can be stressful, confusing and tiring, especially if you're a teenager and you don't want to miss that party or hot date to see Mum or Dad. It can be difficult ordering your life around outings with one parent, while trying to keep both parents happy.

It's usual for contact with younger children to be agreed between the split parents at their convenience. However, as a teenager who is maturing and becoming increasingly independent, with important friendships and the stress of exams looming large, it's reasonable for you to want some say in contact decisions. Handling parents and emotions in the very sensitive area of contact is tricky; it takes patience and understanding:

Tips on handling contact

■ If contact is haphazard, explain to Mum and Dad how important it is for you to see your absent parent on a regular basis. It's vital for a child of any age to have consistency and stability, so you need to know (in advance) when you're seeing each parent. If no one is making hard decisions, take a calendar or diary to Mum and Dad separately and look at dates and times when you can visit. Factor in out-of-school/-college activities, part-time jobs and other commitments and make them aware of future social events. Try to make it a practical exercise rather than an emotional issue. It's not ideal if you get involved in this process uninvited but sometimes it's the only way to initiate it.

■ If Mum or Dad is reluctant to make contact arrangements there may be an underlying justifiable cause – your welfare and safety – so don't push it too hard until you know the facts. If you believe it's because Mum or Dad doesn't want you to see the other parent you may have to tackle it with her/him. Try not to accuse or rant (see Chapter 3). Gently remind your parent that their relationship with one another is separate from your relationship with them and with the other parent. It's best for you if you continue to have two parents in your life.

■ Don't feel guilty about not being able to keep up your relationship with the parent you're not living with. If distance and availability are a problem, just work round what is possible and see them when you can. There's no point having unreasonable expectations about contact, and then beating yourself up over it. Often, in the early days of a breakup when parents are trying to create separate lives, it may not be possible to have regular access to the absent parent. Work and living arrangements may be temporary, and finances may

'I want to spend time with Dad and I miss him, but sometimes it's really hard to go away for the weekend when there's stuff going on at home. I've missed sports matches, parties, sleepovers and treats with friends in the last three years. It's been OK but I think I can probably talk to him and Mum now and ask if they can sort out other dates so I can be with my mates.'

Lucy, 13

be stretched. Try to keep in touch via email, snail mail, text messaging and phonecalls. If you can't afford credits for your mobile, ask the absent parent to buy some for you – but do let the parent you are living with know what's going on so they don't feel you're making contact behind their back.

■ Often the trickiest aspect of contact is changeover. Just remember how awkward it is for your Mum and Dad to encounter one another regularly. They've chosen to live apart because they no longer want a partnership, yet they are obliged to maintain a relationship because of the children. It can be difficult for them to handle it, especially at first when they may feel hurt and bitter. However, it does get better with time and is handled better if all arrangements are agreed in advance and any discussions or arguments are conducted outside changeover time.

■ Don't be afraid to let parents know your feelings and how their behaviour is making you feel. It's a new experience for them too and they may not be confident how best to handle it. Help them make the right decisions by discussing what's acceptable and preferable for you – as coolly and calmly as possible!

Statement of Arrangements

When a petition for divorce is filed, if there are any children who are under 16 or in full-time education, a Statement of Arrangements must be filed with the divorce petition. This shows which parent the children will live with and the contact arrangements for the absent parent.

This is often an area of major battles: one parent may want too much or too little contact; or the resident parent may use contact as a weapon against their ex-partner. Young people can sometimes feel like pawns being played according to parents' decisions. However, the court is very clear that the interests of children have to come first (see Chapter 5) and this is the basis on which all parents should approach these arrangements.

It's a fact that children often show distress around the time of meetings with a non-resident parent. Unless there is evidence of harm or abuse, it may be because you want and need more, regular, contact. Sometimes the stress is a result of where the contact takes place. It's awkward for one parent to go to the home of an ex-partner to pick up or deliver a child, and parents may be reluctant to leave children with an ex and his/her new partner. Also, you may feel uncomfortable in this situation. Contact centres can provide a solution because they are neutral venues where non-resident parents can spend time with their children (see Resources for more information).

LOSING CONTACT

Sometimes it's not in the best interests of children to see a parent regularly. If a child is at risk of violence, abuse, neglect or criminal activity, social services, the Family Court and even the police can get involved. But it's usually in the best interests of children to have regular contact with both parents and there is a trend towards granting joint

FACT BOX

Research shows that children who have another adult (such as a grandparent or other relative) to fill some of the functions of the absent parent have fewer problems than children who have no substitute for the absent parent.
Source: P R Amato, 'Life-span adjustment of children to their parents' divorce', *Children and Divorce*, vol. 4, no. 1 (Spring 1994)

residency, where a child has two homes and spends equal time with each parent.

If you're concerned about losing contact with the parent you don't live with, you need to assert influence on both your parents. You may not know the full circumstances, but talk to them and find out what's going to happen in the future. Even a young adult may not have the authority to influence parents' wishes or plans for contact. You may have to take advice on how to proceed or ask an adult to make your case for you. (Often grandparents can help in this situation – see Chapter 6 for more information.)

If you want a neutral representative, ask a trusted family friend or contact the organisations listed in the Resources section for help. If you want to talk to a trained counsellor, groups like the National Youth Advocacy Service or Relate can put you in touch with someone in your area (see Resources for details).

You may sometimes feel that you don't want to see a parent, especially if there is conflict between Mum and Dad. Visits are not always going to be perfect and some fathers especially have to learn how to parent again. Getting into a comfortable routine takes time and juggling two lives takes practice. Give it time, put in some effort and keep lines of communication open; it does get easier.

CHAPTER EIGHT

DAD'S DATING!
Stepfamilies/ extended families

Frequently, just as you settle into life with a lone parent, another adult is added to the equation. If you have spent years living with Mum or Dad, or have an especially close relationship with one of your parents, it can be difficult to accept that another person is now part of his or her life – and yours.

'I just look back on the divorce now as part of my life, like primary school. My Stepdad's cool; I don't even mind having a stepfamily. There are just more people around to get to know. I've even got a little stepbrother who I really like. I don't have any less of a relationship with Mum, so it's added to my life, not taken anything away.'

Maud, 16

Statistics show that for the majority of lone parents, singledom is a temporary state, lasting on average five years. If you're a teenager and you've been with Mum or Dad for that long on your own, you may find it difficult when someone else starts to figure in her or his affections.

But for a parent, a relationship with a peer and with a child is not usually an either/or situation. You may find that some attention and affection is diverted from you to another man or woman – especially during the first few heady months – but Mum or Dad don't love you any less.

A parent can juggle life and love effectively enough to include children, boyfriends or girlfriends and, if it comes to it, stepchildren and new children too. Yes, it's a Herculean task to spread time, energy and love around to make a new lover and children all feel special all the time, but many exhausted and frustrated parents and step-parents do it every day. Just because they don't always achieve complete family inclusivity, it doesn't mean they don't want to.

If you've gone through the painful transition of a family breakup it's understandable that once you settle into your new routines with Mum and Dad you want everything to remain the same forever. But think about it: Mum or Dad wanted a divorce for another chance of happiness, so the chances are he or she will want to date. As a teenager you'll be moving on, wanting to get on with your own life – well, parents want to do that too.

'Mum or Dad wanted a divorce for another chance of happiness, so the chances are he or she will want to date.'

If Mum or Dad has a boyfriend or girlfriend they may have been seeing during the time they were together, try not to get angry. There may have been other things about the marriage that led your parent to stray, so don't blame the third party. Give your parent the chance of a relationship.

Seeing a parent getting dolled up for a night out or excited over a new lover can make you squeamish. Recognising that parents may want to do the same things you want to may just be too much. But remember, new relationships tend to be more intense and more sexual, so accept the phase that Mum or Dad is going through.

> 'Just as your parents step back and let you make your own mistakes in life (and learn from them), you need to give them space too.'

Often, parents who have been in long-term relationships haven't dated for years and may be just as nervous as you or your mates when seeing someone new. Sometimes you won't know what's going on and sometimes there may be too much information, but if it's handled well, these dual experiences (a generation apart) can bring you closer together. Some older teenagers – especially daughters – can help parents work out the rules of the dating game.

On the other hand, parents may not always welcome the intrusion into their personal life and criticising a parent's new partner is a rocky road to travel. Not everyone makes the best choices in love and it can be painful for you to see Mum or Dad falling for (who you think is) the wrong man or woman. But just as they step back and let you make your own mistakes in life (and learn from them), you need to give them space too.

GETTING SERIOUS

For many teenagers, especially those who have had Mum or Dad to themselves for a few years, the shock of having to share a parent and a home with another adult may be overwhelming.

The relationship between boys and their mothers can be especially tricky: you may have been the 'alpha male' in the home until all of a sudden Mum's loved up and there's some other man's shaving things in the bathroom. And if you've always been Daddy's Little Girl, it can be uncomfortable to see him cuddling another woman.

If you are against having a stepfather or are convinced you're going to end up with a wicked stepmother, run through some reality checks before you leap to conclusions:

- If the man/woman in question wasn't going out with Mum/Dad, how would you really rate them as a person? Is it their Stepdad/Stepmum status you're feeling angry with, or them?
- If you can't bear Mum/Dad having a boyfriend/girlfriend, is it because you genuinely think they've picked the wrong person? Or don't you want them to have another adult relationship because you want them to get back with your other parent?

'He seems to think he can tell me what to do, but he hasn't got the right. He isn't my real Dad.'

Alison, 15 (Source: ChildLine)

- Do you hate the way Mum/Dad slobbers over her/his boyfriend/girlfriend because you don't like her/his new partner or because you don't have anyone to go out with at the moment?
- Do you resent Mum/Dad a boyfriend/girlfriend because you think they're making a fool of themselves? Or do you just wish it was you and Mum/Dad once again because you were the centre of her/his attention?

Just remember:

- Mum/Dad is entitled to a loving adult relationship
- You're never too old to fall in love and fancy someone!
- In your eyes, no one's ever going to be right for Mum or Dad
- Your relationship with Mum/Dad is completely separate from any they have with anyone else – there's enough love to go around
- The happier Mum/Dad is, the less hassle it'll be for you!

'It feels wrong when I'm having fun with Dad and his new wife, when I think of Mum by herself.'

Alice, 15 (Source: ChildLine)

FEAR OF THE UNKNOWN

The biggest problem is imagining how your life might change – fantasising about the wicked Stepmother/Stepfather you'll have to put up with, and assuming the worst. Remember, fear of the unknown is usually worse than the reality, so it's important to get to know a prospective Stepmum/Stepdad as a person – don't believe the stereotype. Here are a few of the things you might be thinking ...

■ 'She's making up to Dad because he's got a house and a good job.' (*Yes, but don't forget, he's got emotional baggage and children as well!*)

■ 'He's only with Mum because she's vulnerable and needy.' (*Maybe Mum needs a bit of love and affection and as long as there's care and respect in the relationship, isn't that OK?*)

■ 'She's serious about Dad and he's not ready for a relationship yet.' (*If you're sure of your information and observations, have a quiet word with Dad.*)

■ 'He's obviously not after a serious relationship and Mum will get hurt.' (*Maybe Mum isn't after a serious relationship with him either. She is entitled to some fun. If you've got to know him and you feel Mum isn't seeing the real person, chat to her calmly about how you feel.*)

■ 'She's only nice to me because she wants to score points with Dad.' (*She's making an effort, so give her the benefit of the doubt until you know her well or you have proof it's a sham!*)

■ 'He'll start asking to be called Daddy and will make me change my surname, or even adopt me.' (*While your father is alive, you only have one Dad. Most step-parents these days do not expect to take on the role of biological mother or father, especially if you have a close relationship with your absent parent. Ask your Stepmum or Stepdad if you can call them by their Christian name. You may find that after a while you automatically begin to refer to her/him as Stepmum or Stepdad. Children usually only take on a new surname if the parent and step-parent marry and there's no contact with the absent parent. You can discuss this with your parents, but it's really up to you what you want to do. Nowadays it's rare for a parent to adopt a stepchild unless the biological mother or father is dead.*)

■ 'She wants to live in our house and take over our lives.' (*If she's committed to a relationship with your Dad (and you) she'll want to contribute to creating a new life for the whole family. Try to go with the flow for a while and support her ideas. If they conflict with yours, quietly and thoughtfully put across your point of view.*)

■ 'He wants me and Mum to live with him but it'll be his house with his rules and it won't be my home.' (*It's generous of your stepfather to want to share his home with you and your mother. Moving to someone else's home is more difficult than moving to neutral territory; a new home for all of you. But it will always take time and negotiation to adapt to new surroundings. You can feel it's your home by having some say in what goes on in it, but everyone has to abide by house rules, no matter who sets them.*)

It's obviously going to be different from how it was before, so try to have realistic expectations. It's complicated and it takes time to adjust: all family life is about compromise.

FACT BOX

More than a third of parents are raising children alone or within stepfamilies. The strain is leading to increasing tension and conflict, with the financial and time pressures caused by 'families within families' taking a heavy toll.
Source: Mintel

Any group of people thrown together in a house are bound to rub along sometimes and clash madly at others – just look at *Big Brother*! When accepting anyone into your life you first have to go through a process of getting to know them, starting to trust them and establishing boundaries with them.

You need to spend time with a step-parent to get on their wavelength. It's all very well being together as a new family, but you need time on your own with Stepmum or Stepdad. Try to get to know the person first and forget about their status.

Being a stepfather or stepmother can be a thankless task. Often they find they are blamed for everything and feel pressure to be perfect and get things right all the time while juggling a new relationship, a new home and a new family.

Where to draw the line

It's always a good idea to give people the benefit of the doubt when judging new relationships. Home life with a teenager can be fraught enough! But there is some behaviour that shouldn't be tolerated:

- If a step-parent encroaches on your space and privacy. Your things – like post and belongings – are yours, and your ownership and privacy should be respected. If there's enough room, you should at least have the sanctuary of your bedroom.
- If a step-parent touches or looks at you inappropriately or makes improper suggestions. Speak to your parent as soon as you can or go to a relation or trusted adult for advice. If you feel in danger, call social services or the police.
- If a step-parent or parent tells known lies or is aggressive and rude about your other parent. Calmly tell them you are not prepared to listen, and walk away from the situation. If it keeps happening, speak to a third party about intervening on your behalf.
- If a step-parent or parent asks you to spy on the other parent, or vice versa. It's difficult, but try to keep your two lives separate, and don't take sides.
- If a step-parent or parent uses you as a go-between to negotiate contact. As an older child you should be included in discussions

about contact but it is up to your two parents to agree a provisional plan or arrangement. You shouldn't end up as the ping pong ball batting between them.

■ If a step-parent denies you arranged contact with your birth parent. There can be pressure to be the 'perfect new family' and a step-parent may feel that contact with your absent parent does not fit in with this image. It's important for you to stay in contact with both parents if at all possible, and having a new life and new family with one of them shouldn't prevent this.

Research shows that family structure isn't as important as living with someone who cares about you. Many people live within extended families and are cared for by grandparents, aunts and uncles; Mum and Dad don't have to be your primary carers. The fact is that having someone who loves you and looks out for you – whether they're a biological parent or not – is what really matters.

THE FAMILY MOLE

It may not necessarily be your step-parent, but your Mum or Dad's reaction to them, you have problems with. Often, one parent settles down with a new partner while the other remains alone. This can complicate your relationship with your parent, especially if Mum or Dad has made a new life with someone they were seeing during the marriage. Being in this situation can be unpleasant for you and difficult to handle for everyone.

'Every time I go out with Dad, he quizzes me about Mum and my new Stepdad. I feel like a spy.'

Alex, 16 (Source: ChildLine)

'My Stepmum is not a nice person; even her own mother told us she was "unbalanced". Once my Stepmum told me my Mum was "sick in the head". She says she knows her better than anyone because they were best friends for years!'

Chloe, 16

Parents don't mean to make life difficult for their children, but endless accusations, recriminations, anger and bitterness can make life a misery. Split loyalties and emotional blackmail can also mean that you don't feel there's anyone you can talk to about it. If you feel under pressure and unable to change anything, do think about getting someone to speak to your parents on your behalf.

There's nothing wrong with letting your parents know their actions are making you miserable. If one parent expects you to be a spy or a go-between or to take sides, don't be afraid to tell them they are behaving badly and putting unfair pressure on you. You can make your feelings clear by answering their questions with: 'If you want to know, ask Mum/Dad'. Sometimes warring parents can load teenage children with adult responsibility but not give them the adult respect that goes with it. Unfortunately, step-parents can bring out the worst in hurt adults, but usually the hurt diminishes after time.

NEW LIFE, NEW FAMILY

Stepfamilies can be a joy or a pain – depending on how you view the addition of new family members to your home life. Having a stepbrother or stepsister can give you opportunity to experience new relationships that are often rewarding (especially if you are an only child).

Stepchildren have to accept the fact that being connected to new people in a stepfamily is just another kind of relationship. Like any relationship – at college, at work or socially – you need to adapt. You will probably feel resentful, perhaps even jealous and frequently irritated, but that's what it's like. It will be unfamiliar and awkward for a while, but it will get better and easier. You never know – you might actually enjoy it!

Stepfamily survival tactics

■ Parents and stepfamilies aren't mind-readers, so they might not realise how they make you feel. You might not get your own way, but if you tell them straight, you can try to find a compromise.
■ Try to avoid sounding petulant (eg 'I don't like having to move in with them' or 'I don't like them staying here'). Try a more reasonable approach, like 'Moving in with them makes me feel ...' or 'When they stay here I feel ...'

'I've always wanted brothers and sisters and now I have an older stepbrother who's really cool and a stepsister who's the same age. We're more like friends really, except I share her home when I stay with my Dad. I sleep in her room and it's OK. My Stepmum even let us choose new beds and sheets.'

Lucy, 13

FACT BOX

Support while the stepfamily is being formed may be as important as support following separation. Young children in stepfamilies seem to fare better, possibly because it is easier to adapt to a new family structure at an age when they have had a relatively short period of living with either both or just one birth parent.

Source: Joseph Rowntree Foundation

■ If the presence of step-siblings makes you feel increasingly less significant in your parent's life, try to negotiate some special time with him or her. Create a routine of regular trips or time when you do something you both enjoy, alone together. When you approach Mum or Dad, try not to sound needy or demanding; instead say something like, 'I know this may sound silly, but I feel you have less time for me nowadays and I miss our chats.'

■ If you just can't grab Mum or Dad for a heart-to-heart, email her/him or leave a letter in the bedroom. Explain the message by saying: 'I wanted to write to you to get my thoughts in order and to keep emotions out of the communication.'

■ Don't force friendships with new step-siblings. Ask them (nicely) to back off if they're too overbearing. Let it happen gradually – just like any other friendship. If you feel they're too much in your face, be honest: don't make excuses, fob them off, or ignore them completely. Younger children, especially, need gentle handling; it's difficult for them too.

- If step-siblings want too much of your time or attention, tell them you need to study, go out with your friends or spend some time alone. But make an opportunity to spend time with them and agree it in advance.
- Keep your two lives with two parents as separate as possible.

'It's hard getting to know lots of people all at once.'

Michael, 12 (Source: ChildLine)

NEW FAMILY, NEW CHILDREN

Life changes again when more children are added to the family. It can be difficult to accept that Mum or Dad has children younger and more needy than you. Teenagers, especially, can feel pushed out of the family and sometimes even get pushed out of the home when half-brothers or sisters are born.

'If I have kids I hope they don't feel like how I felt ... disowned ... so unhappy. I felt nobody wanted me in their house.'

Becky, 16 (Source: YoungMinds)

For many, it can be a joy to be involved in the everyday care and upbringing of a new sibling, but for those still smarting from the diversion of attention, it's rubbing salt into the wound. Older children are often given the task of being 'helper' to the parent and step-parent and are given almost adult responsibilities with younger children, especially if there is a large age gap. This can be a difficult role for a teenager, especially if it affects your social life or prevents you from studying.

> *'My Dad's such a good father to his new daughter, he was never like that with me or my brothers. She's his princess and I always wanted to be his princess.'*
>
> **Chloe, 16**

ADOPTING A STEPCHILD

Stepchild adoption is not common in the UK. Adoption is always looked at with the best interests of the child foremost and, as with joint residency, the courts feel that whenever possible it's best for the child to maintain a relationship with both biological parents. However, this isn't always possible and there are occasions when a parent and step-parent feel it would be best to adopt.

FACT BOX

Adoption figures peaked at 25,000 in 1968, fell markedly in the mid-1970s and have remained fairly constant at about 5000 per year in the last ten years. Step-parent adoptions peaked at almost 15,000 in 1974 and have also fallen markedly since.

Source: Mind

Sometimes the driving force behind the adoption application is the parents' wish to form a complete family; but adoption isn't always the right solution for the stepchild.

What people may not consider is the adoption process and what may result from it. Frequently, a parent who has had no contact with the

FACT BOX

In England and Wales both the natural parent and step-parent adopt a stepchild together. In Scotland the step-parent alone can adopt the child with the natural parent's consent. If the parent and step-parent marry they will have to wait one to two years before applying for adoption.

Source: www.adoption.org.uk

'It's weird to hear myself say that having step-parents and step-siblings is a bonus gained from my parents' divorce. My life seemed to be falling apart. But now I've gained another Dad, lots of brothers and sisters and Mum and Dad get on fine. We've all helped each other along.'

Emma, 16 (Source: YoungMinds)

stepchild comes into contact with the child. An absent mother or father who is – or once was – married to the resident parent has to give consent for the adoption. A mother or father with whom you have had no real relationship may meet you, briefly spend some time with you, then walk out of your life again, which can make you feel doubly rejected.

CHAPTER NINE:

ENDNOTE

When a family breaks up it's bewildering and shocking for many children. No matter what age you are, the process of family separation and making a new life is disruptive and hard work. It can take time – sometimes years – to recover and adapt.

It's proven that very young children cope well, adapting quickly to the new situation. Young adults who have moved away from home also accept the changes in parents' relationships with a better, adult-to-adult, understanding. However, those who are frequently seen as being the most able to cope and move on (the 13–18 age group) are often the ones who get into trouble. And that can be trouble in the literal sense, as sadness, anger and frustration are acted out in defiant and disorderly behaviour.

Teenagers have a lot going on: exams, study, work, new relationships, new hormones and a developing sense of a new self. Many young people won't admit to needing their family during these years, but for all children security is important. When chaos at home is mixed in with everything else in the adolescent experience, life can feel unstable.

Experts accept that the stresses of modern life and the process of adolescence make the teenage years a vulnerable time. Look at the mental health of Britain's young people – suicide, self-harm and depression figures are rising.

Decades ago it was felt that divorce was best for the family if left until after the children had been brought up. When divorce was still taboo and little long-term research had been conducted, the belief was that teenagers could cope better with a family breakup than young children. For years, warring and depressed Mums and Dads stayed in bad marriages 'for the sake of the kids'; then dropped the bombshell on unprepared, delicate teenagers.

But for teenagers the dynamics of divorce can be different to parents' assumptions. Issues that are key to a healthy separation may not always be top of your parents' list of considerations. For example:

- You may want to know the truth about Mum and Dad's relationship and feel mature enough to understand what went on and what's happening now.
- You may feel you should have greater powers of influencing, and that decision-making should be more inclusive.
- You may need your priorities, relationships and routines to be valued. Teenagers don't want to have the same arrangements and assumptions applied to them as to younger siblings.
- You may want to be able to cry on someone's shoulder and still be Mummy or Daddy's Princess or Baby. Just because you're nearly an adult, you don't want to be treated like one *all* the time.
- As a young adult you don't want everyone to assume that it's your responsibility to support younger siblings' emotional needs – or your parents'.

How these wishes are expressed comes down to your relationship with your parents and how they handle the process. Studies show that divorce and family breakup are not necessarily detrimental to children in the long term. What makes the difference between children of split parents coming through and growing up healthy, and those who are scarred by the experience, is down to how it's handled.

That's a huge responsibility for parents. They have to manage all the practical aspects of a breakup as well as everyone's emotional needs, just when they are at their most vulnerable and confused. It's understandable that Mum and Dad don't always say or do 'the right thing' in these circumstances. There's no training for getting divorced or being a step-parent; adults have to muddle though, making mistakes and learning from them. One of the difficult roles teenagers have is helping that learning process as well as looking after their own needs.

'You'll hurt and wish it wasn't happening to you. But it's happening to lots of people. It'll make you a stronger person in the end.'

This book should have given you some guidance in some areas of difficulty. It won't be difficult all the time and you won't need help all the time, but contained in *Family Breakups* are tactics, advice and information that just might help you handle the whole thing better.

We will leave you with some advice from the experts on how to get through a family breakup:

A Counsellor with ChildLine says:

- 'For life to get from horrible to being great again involves tricky times. Find a middle way and try to avoid extreme emotions and reactions. Remember, feelings are often the consequence of irrational thought.

- 'Young people are incredibly important within a family and have rights. You *can* ask for your needs to be met; don't be afraid to acknowledge your feelings. If you can't get through to your parents, talk to someone else. Use other adults to negotiate for you.'

Paula Hall, Young People's Counsellor and Sex and Relationships Therapist, Relate, says:

- 'Take one day at a time. Today it might feel as if your whole life is turned upside down and things will never be right again. But many thousands of young people do survive their parents' divorce, so just take things slowly and trust that everything will settle down in time.

- 'Your parents still love you and do want the very best for you, but they also have to look after their own needs and think about their future. Sometimes that means you're going to clash and argue, but try to hang on to the fact that even though circumstances are changing, their love for you isn't.'

Chloe, 16, says:

- 'It's easy to think you're somehow to blame for what has happened. You're not. Mum and Dad have their own relationship, which is different to how they feel about you. They love you more than anything. Remember that.

- 'It's not the end of the world, so live with it. Don't rebel against it; it makes everything more complicated.

- 'Keep level-headed and don't jump to conclusions. Don't take to heart everything that's said in the heat of the moment.

- 'Don't side with one parent and don't lose contact with one parent.
- 'If there are really bad times, just remember it's going to be hard; you'll hurt and wish it wasn't happening to you. But it's happening to lots of people. It'll make you a stronger person in the end.'

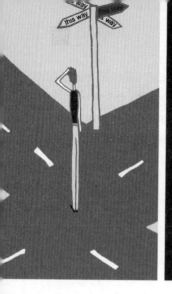

GENERAL ADVICE, SUPPORT AND INFORMATION FOR YOUNG PEOPLE

BBC

Tel: 0800 110 100 (One Lifeline, 24 hours)

Web: www.bbc.co.uk/relationships *or* www.bbc.co.uk/radio1/onelife

These websites have many different pages on relationships, family and health that may be helpful.

Channel 4

Web: www.channel4.com/health

Helpful material on relationships, family and health.

ChildLine

Tel: 0800 1111 (Free 24-hour helpline)

Web: www.childline.org.uk

The national helpline for young people in trouble or danger. There is also assistance for parents.

Citizens Advice Bureau (CAB)

Web: www.adviceguide.org.uk

Provides free, confidential and independent advice via its website and network of advice centres throughout the country – see www.citizensadvice.org.uk or look in the telephone directory to find your local branch.

Connexions Direct

Helpline: 080 8001 3219

Web: www.connexions-direct.com

Provides information and advice for 13- to 19-year-olds on a range of matters from health and relationships to housing and careers. Connexions counsellors are available to give personal advice through your school or college.

Kidscape

2 Grosvenor Gardens

London SW1W 0DH

Tel: 020 7730 3300

Helpline: 08451 205 204

Fax: 020 7730 7081

Email: webinfo@kidscape.org.uk

Web: www.kidscape.org.uk

The bullying and abuse charity that offers help and information to children and parents through its counsellors and website.

Mind

Tel: 020 8519 2122

Web: www.mind.org.uk

Menal health charity with over 200 local associations in England and Wales.

NCH

Helpline: 08457 626579 (lo-call; Monday to Friday 9am to 5pm)
Web: www.nch.org.uk and www.itsnotyourfault.org
The charity that helps young people affected by poverty,
homelessness, disability and abuse. The **It's not your fault** *website,*
run by NCH, is aimed specifically at those going through family break-
up and has separate sections for children, teenagers and parents.

NSPCC

NSPCC Child Protection Helpline
42 Curtain Road
London EC2A 3NH
Tel: 0808 800 5000 (24-hour helpline)
Web: www.nspcc.org.uk and www.there4me.com
The NSPCC is a child protection charity and provides advice and
counselling. Its **There 4 me** *website is aimed specifically at 12- to 16-*
year-olds.

Relate

Tel: 0845 456 1310
Web: www.relate.org.uk
Offers counselling for couples facing separation or divorce, and
information sessions to help parents manage the effect on children. It
also offers family counselling at a charge and free counselling in
some areas. Call the number given above to find your nearest free
counselling service. Relate Direct offers email or over-the-phone
counselling at a charge. Book an appointment on 0845 130 4016
(Monday to Friday 9am to 5pm).

The Samaritans

PO Pox 9090
Stirling FK8 2SA

Tel: 08457 909090 (UK); 1850 609090 (Republic of Ireland)
Email: jo@samaritans.org
Web: www.samaritans.org.uk
*Offers a confidential listening service every day of the year, for anyone
troubled, despairing or suicidal.*

YoungMinds

48–50 St John Street
London EC1M 4DG
Tel: 020 7336 8445
Email: info@youngminds.org.uk
Web: www.youngminds.org.uk
*The mental health charity for children and young people, offering
advice for troubled teenagers and parents. Offers a Parents'
Information Service, tel: 0800 018 2138 (Monday and Friday 10am
to 1pm; Tuesday to Thursday 1pm to 4 pm; Wednesday evenings
6pm to 8pm).*

Youth Access

1–2 Taylors Yard
67 Alderbrook Road
London SW12 8AD
Tel: 020 8772 9900
Email: admin@youthaccess.org.uk
Web: www.youthaccess.org.uk
*Youth Access is the national membership organisation for young
people's information, advice, counselling and support services.
Although it is unable to offer support direct to young people, its website
includes a directory of over 300 relevant organisations that do.*

YouthNet Uk

Web: www.thesite.org.uk/sexandrelationships/familiesandfriends/family.

A *charity that runs* **The Site**, *a website aimed at young people with articles about relationships, breakups, and how to cope when your parents split up.*

DIVORCE
Department for Constitutional Affairs
Web: www.dca.gov.uk/family/divleaf.htm
Offers useful leaflets for parents and children going through divorce.

Divorce
Web: www.divorce.co.uk
This website (hosted by law firm Mills-Reeve) provides comprehensive information on all aspects of divorce.

Divorce Aid
Web: www.divorceaid.co.uk
A useful self-help and support website for families going through separation and divorce, which includes pages for teenagers.

National Youth Agency
Web: www.youthinformation.com
This website offers up-to-date practical information and advice for young people on love and sex, law and justice, and divorce.

THE LAW AND SOCIAL SERVICES
CAFCASS
8th Floor
South Quay Plaza 3
189 Marsh Wall
London E14 9SH

Tel: 020 7510 7000

Email: webenquiries@cafcass.gov.uk

Web: www.cafcass.gov.uk

CAFCASS (Children and Family Court Advisory and Support Service) looks after the interests of children involved in family proceedings. It works with children and their families, and then advises the courts on what it considers to be in the child's best interests. The website offers lots of easily understood information.

Child Abduction Unit, Lord Chancellor's Office

Tel: 020 7911 7047 (Monday to Friday 9am to 5pm)

Fax: 020 7911 7248

Email: enquiries@offsol.gsi.gov.uk

Web: www.offsol.demon.co.uk

Responsible for administering the work of the European Conventions on Child Abduction. The website has a valuable series of links to other resources, both in the UK and overseas.

Children's Legal Centre

University of Essex

Wivenhoe Park

Colchester

Essex CO4 3SQ

Tel: 0845 456 6811 (National Education Law Advice Line, Monday to Friday 9.30am to 5.00pm)

Email: nel@essex.ac.uk (the centre will call back within 24 hours)

Web: www.childrenslegalcentre.com

A charity concerned with law and policy affecting children and young people. The centre operates a national advice line on behalf of the Legal Services Commission. It runs the **National Education Law Advice Line***, which provides up to 30 minutes of free legal advice and information, and the* **Education Legal Advocacy Unit***, which* *provides free legal advice and representation to children and/or parents with concerns relating to schools or Local Education Authorities (LEAs).*

Essex Young person's and Children's Advocacy Network (EYpCAN)

Tel: 0800 783 2187
Web: www.giveusavoice.org
Provides a service for young people in Essex, but their website also provides up-to-date information and advice.

Family Rights Group (FRG)

The Print House
18 Ashwin Street
London E8 3DL
Tel: 0800 731 1696 (Monday to Friday 10am to 12pm and 1.30pm to 3.30pm)
Web: www.frg.org.uk
The group is a registered charity and provides advice and support for families whose children are involved with social services. FRG works to improve the services received by families. It has a free, confidential advice line.

National Family Mediation (NFM)

Tel: 0117 904 2825
Email: general@nfm.org.uk
Web: www.nfm.u-net.com
A network of over 60 local not-for-profit Family Mediation Services in England and Wales offering help to couples, married or unmarried, who are separating or divorcing.

National Youth Advocacy Service (NYAS)

Tel: 0800 616101
Email: help@nyas.net

Web: www.nyas.net
*A children's charity offering socio-legal advocacy services to children,
young people and parents.*

Resolution
Tel: 01689 850227
Email: info@sfla.org.uk
Web: www.sfla.org.uk
*This is the online portal for the Solicitors' Family Law Association
(SFLA), a nationwide association of over 5000 solicitors specialising in
family law.*

PARENTS AND FAMILIES
General and shared parenting
Association for Shared Parenting
Tel: 01789 751157
Email: spring.cott@btopenworld.com
Web: www.sharedparenting.org.uk
*Has regional branches and offers help and support to parents,
grandparents and relations of a child involved in a divorce or
separation.*

Both Parents Forever
Tel: 01689 854343
*Produces information packs explaining individuals' rights and legal
precedents regarding divorce, separation and care proceedings.*

National Association of Child Contact Centres (NACCC)
Tel: 0845 450 0280
Fax: 0845 450 0420

Email: contact@naccc.org.uk
Web: http://naccc.org.uk
Promotes safe child contact within a national framework of Child Contact Centres.

National Society for Children and Family Contact (NSCFC)

Tel: 0870 766 8596 (Helpline)
Web: www.childrenneedfathers.org
Has a manifesto to promote change in English family law in the interests of children. It offers advice for children, parents and grandparents going through a family breakup.

Parentline Plus

Tel: 0808 800 2222 (24-hour helpline; textphone 0800 783 6783)
Web: www.parentlineplus.org.uk
A charity offering support to anyone parenting a child.

Lone parents

Gingerbread

Tel: 020 7488 9300
Helpline: 0800 018 4318 (Monday to Friday 9am to 5pm)
Email: advice@gingerbread.org.uk
Web: www.gingerbread.org.uk
Provides day-to-day support and practical help for lone parents and their children via a national network of local self-help groups.

National Council for the Divorced and Separated (NCDS)

Tel: 07041 478 120 (6pm to 9pm)
Web: www.ncds.org.uk
A voluntary organisation that aims to promote an active social life for its members. There are NCDS branches throughout the British Isles.

One Parent Families

Tel: 0800 018 5026 (Free helpline, Monday to Friday 9am to 5pm,
Wednesday 9am to 8pm)
Web: www.oneparentfamilies.org.uk
*Provides information about the laws and benefits system of England
and Wales.*

Single Parents' Action Network

Tel: 0117 951 4231
Web: www.singleparents.org.uk *or* www.spanuk.org.uk
*A multi-racial organisation run by single parents working to improve
conditions for one-parent families.*

Fathers

Families Need Fathers

Tel: 08707 607496 (Monday to Friday 6pm to 10pm)
Web: www.fnf.org.uk
*Represents non-resident parents and their children. It is concerned
with keeping parents and children in contact after family breakdown. A
national network of volunteers provides advice and support.*

Fathers Direct

Herald House
Lamb's Passage
Bunhill Row
London EC1Y 8TQ
Tel: 0845 634 1328
Email: mail@fathersdirect.com
Web: www.fathersdirect.com
*A charity founded in 1999 by professionals with expertise in social
work, family policy, business development and communications. It's
the national information centre on fatherhood.*

Mothers
Mothers Apart from their Children
BM Problems

London WC1N 3XX

Email: enquiries@matchmothers.org

Web: www.matchmothers.org

This is a nationwide support network for women living apart from their children.

Grandparents
Grandparents Association
The Stow

Harlow

Essex CM20 3AG

Tel: 01279 444964 (Helpline)

Email: info@grandparents-association.org.uk

Web: www.grandparents-association.co.uk

Gives advice, information and support to grandparents of children affected by a divorce or separation.

Stepfamilies
ChildLine
Web: www.childline.org.uk/stepfamilies.asp

StepFamilies
Web: www.stepfamilies.co.uk

Website providing information and sharing opportunities.

ADOPTION
Adoption Information Line
Tel: 0800 783 4086 (Freephone)

Web: www.adoption.org.uk
Provides adoption-related information.

Department of Health

Web: www.doh.gov.uk/adoption
The government's official adoption site.

HOUSING

Shelter

Tel: 0808 800 4444
Web: www.shelter.org.uk
A housing charity offering advice online. It has an Advice Services Directory covering England, Scotland, Wales and Northern Ireland. There is also a free Housing Advice Helpline open seven days a week from 8am to midnight.

ABUSE

Hidden Hurt

Web: www.hiddenhurt.co.uk
Provides information and advice on domestic violence, including lists of national and regional helpline numbers.

Rape Crisis

Email: info@rapecrisis.org.uk
Web: www.rapecrisis.org.uk
Website offers information and contains contact details of support groups throughout the country.

Victim Support

Tel: 0845 303 0900
Email: supportline@victimsupport.org.uk
Web: www.victimsupport.org.uk
Offers free and confidential support to those affected by crime.

Women's Aid

Web: www.womensaid.org.uk *or* www.thehideout.org.uk (for children and young people)
Has campaigned since 1974 to protect abused women and children and offers information and support.

BOOKS
Non-fiction

The Citizens Advice Handbook, Penguin (Over 600 pages of practical, independent CAB advice.)

The "Which?" Guide to Divorce: Essential Practical Information for Separating Couples, Imogen Clout

The Facts about Divorce, Caroline Evensen Lazo, Simon and Schuster, 1991

Divorce and New Beginnings: A Complete Guide to Recovery, Solo Parenting, Co-parenting and Stepfamilies, Genevieve Clapp

Relate Guide to Step Families, Suzie Hayman

Mike's Lonely Summer: A Child's Guide Through Divorce, Carolyn Nystrom, Lion Publishing, 1986 (A Christian approach.)

It's Not Your Fault: What to Do when Your Parents Divorce, Rosemary Stoves, Piccadilly

Talking Points: Divorce, Anne Charlish, Wayland Publishing

They F*** You Up: How to Survive Family Life, Oliver James, Bloomsbury

Fiction

The Twig Thing, Jan Mark, Puffin Books

It's Not the End of the World, Judy Blume, Pan Piper

The Divorce Express, Paula Danziger, Pan Piper

Two of Everything, Babette Cole, Jonathan Cape

Addictions

An addiction is often a cover-up for a deeper problem. Drugs, alcohol, gambling or even the internet can all seem to offer a way of escaping from problems. But, ultimately, they can become *the* problem and only increase your misery. This book provides the background knowledge you need to understand how and why people become addicted, and offers advice and suggestions on who to turn to if you need help coping with this difficult issue.

Confidence & Self-Esteem

Some people ooze confidence while others hide in the kitchen at parties. But being confident isn't about being the loudest, coolest or most sporty – as long as you are happy being *you*, then your confidence soars. If this sounds like a tall order, don't worry – confidence can be learnt and self-esteem can be boosted, and this book is here to show you how…

The *Real Life Issues* are a series of friendly and supportive self-help guides covering the issues that matter to you.

For more information on the series and to buy:
visit www.trotman.co.uk or call 0870 900 2665

www.trotman.co.uk

Coping with Life

Being a teenager is not easy: everything about you and your life is changing. Developing the body and mind of an adult and having to deal with responsibilities such as GCSEs and A levels can leave you reeling. At a time of such intense activity and transformation it is not surprising if you sometimes feel unable to cope. This book offers a set of guidelines for tackling teenage stresses such as relationships with friends, families, sexual identity and plans for the future.

Eating Disorders

Eating disorders can wreck lives and should be nipped in the bud; what may start out as a need to fit in and feel in control can escalate into hospitalisation. An eating disorder is normally a cover-up for another problem that can be tackled through other means such as counselling or therapy. If you are struggling with your attitude to food or know a friend who is, then this book can give you the facts you need to confront the situation.

The *Real Life Issues* are a series of friendly and supportive self-help guides covering the issues that matter to you.

For more information on the series and to buy:
visit www.trotman.co.uk or call 0870 900 2665

www.trotman.co.uk

Sex & Relationships

Feeling curious about sex and wanting to know more is a natural part of growing up. This book explores and explains sex and relationships and provides the facts you need to be able to make mature decisions. This book takes an open and honest look at sex and provides advice and tips on how to manage relationships – be they with your parents, friends or the opposite sex.

Stress

Stress is a condition that we increasingly hear about. It's a by-product of the action-packed, high-expectation lifestyles of the twenty-first century and a small amount of stress is normal and healthy. But if you find yourself stressed out and unable to cope with certain situations, be it exams, a breakup or family tensions, then it could be time to take a step back and seek help. This book can help you work out if you're suffering from stress and provides tips and techniques to help you relax and put things into perspective.

The *Real Life Issues* are a series of friendly and supportive self-help guides covering the issues that matter to you.

For more information on the series and to buy:
visit www.trotman.co.uk or call 0870 900 2665

www.trotman.co.uk